I0411825

PHYSICAL PROTECTION

U.S. DEPARTMENT OF ENERGY
Office of Health, Safety and Security

PHYSICAL PROTECTION

1. PURPOSE. This Manual establishes requirements for the physical protection of interests under the U.S. Department of Energy's (DOE's) purview ranging from facilities, buildings, Government property, and employees to national security interests such as classified information, special nuclear material (SNM), and nuclear weapons. A graded approach for the protection of the lowest level of government property and layered to the most critical are described in this Manual and its Appendices.

    a. Graded protection requirements for the various interests under DOE's purview may be required and based on best business practices, economic rationale, national security objectives or other rationale.

    b. Not all Departmental interests can be identified within this Manual. Therefore, DOE line management must consider Departmental interests (i.e., all non-national security interests) and develop protection requirements tailored to that particular interest using graded protection measures.

    c. To effect DOE P 470.1, *Integrated Safeguards and Security Management Policy (ISSM)*, dated 5-8-01, sites must integrate physical security protection into DOE operations and according to sound risk management practices. The ISSM is the Department's philosophical approach to the management of the Safeguards and Security (S&S) Program. A principal objective of ISSM is to integrate S&S into management and work practices at all levels based on program line management's risk management-based decisions so missions may be accomplished without security events such as interruption, disruption or compromise.

    d. Physical protection must be integrated with other S&S programs such as program planning and management, protective force, information security, personnel security, and nuclear material control and accountability.

    e. The activities and requirements outside of the S&S Program in the weapons surety, foreign visits and assignments, safety, emergency management, cyber security, intelligence, and counterintelligence programs must also be considered in the implementation of this Manual.

2. CANCELLATIONS. Section A, of DOE M 470.4-2, Chg 1, *Physical Protection Manual*, dated 3-7-06 is canceled. It should be noted that the Safeguards and Security Alarm Management and Control Systems, formally Section B, has become Appendix C of this Manual and thus remains in effect. Cancellation of a Manual does not by itself modify or otherwise affect any contractual obligation to comply with the Manual. Contractor requirement documents (CRDs) that have been incorporated into or attached to a contract remain in effect until the contract is modified to either eliminate requirements that are no longer applicable or substitute a new set of requirements.

3.   APPLICABILITY.

a.   <u>All Departmental Elements</u>. Except for the exclusion in paragraph 3c, this Manual applies to all Departmental elements including those created after the Manual is issued. (Go to http://www.directives.doe.gov/pdfs/reftools/org-list.pdf for the current listing of Departmental elements.)

The Administrator of the National Nuclear Security Administration (NNSA) will ensure that NNSA employees and contractors comply with their respective responsibilities under this Manual.

b.   <u>DOE Contractors</u>.

(1)   Except for the exclusions in paragraph 3c, the CRD, Attachment 1, sets forth the requirements of this Manual that will apply to contracts that include the CRD.

(2)   The CRD must be included in contracts involving responsibilities for administering DOE Physical Security Programs for the purpose of protecting (S&S) interests. The CRD must contain DOE Acquisition Regulation (DEAR) clause 952.204-2, titled Security Requirements.

(3)   Departmental elements must notify contracting officers of affected site/facility management contracts to incorporate this directive into those contracts.

(4)   Once notified, contracting officers are responsible for incorporating this directive into the affected contracts via the Laws, Regulations, and DOE Directives clause of the contracts.

(5)   A violation of the provisions of the CRD relating to the protection and control of Restricted Data or other classified information may result in a civil penalty pursuant to subsection a. of Section 234B of the Atomic Energy Act of 1954 (42 U.S.C. 2282b.). The procedures for the assessment of civil penalties are set forth in Title 10, Code of Federal Regulations (CFR), Part 824, Procedural Rules for the Assessment of Civil Penalties for Classified Information Security Violations.

c.   <u>Exclusion</u>. In accordance with the responsibilities and authorities assigned by Executive Order 12344, codified at 50 USC sections 2406 and 2511, and to ensure consistency throughout the joint Navy and DOE organization of the Naval Nuclear Propulsion Program, the Deputy Administrator for Naval Reactors (Director) will implement and oversee all requirements and practices pertaining to this DOE Manual for activities under the Director's cognizance, as deemed appropriate.

4. <u>SUMMARY</u>. This Manual, identified as the base Manual, is composed of 10 chapters and three appendices that provide direction for planning, implementing, and monitoring the application of physical protection measures. The chapters and appendices describe the procedures and management process applicable to Departmental operating environments. Implementation of these procedures should be accomplished under an approved security plan, as described in DOE M 470.4-1, that describes an integrated, performance–based approach to site security.

    a.   Chapters I through X provide the baseline requirements applicable to all Departmental facilities and sites.

    b.   The appendices describe the mandatory requirements specifically oriented to Category III and IV SNM, protection of nuclear components, fuel elements and Category I and II SNM, nuclear weapons, test devices and S&S Alarm Management and Control Systems requirements.

    c.   Attachment 1 contains the CRD which provides detailed requirements for DOE contractors consistent with this Manual.

    d.   Attachment 2 describes the Department's security badge policy that is consistent with Homeland Security Presidential Directive 12 (HSPD-12).

    e.   Appendix C cites the Safeguards and Security Alarm Management and Control Systems (SAMACS) requirements used in the protection of Category I and II quantities at SNM facilities installed and operational after January 1, 2008.

5. <u>DEVIATIONS</u>. Deviations from national regulations, including the Code of Federal Regulations and national-level policies, are subject to the deviation process of the governing document rather than the DOE deviation process. This directive conveys no authority to deviate from law. Requests for deviations from requirements specific to DOE, including this Manual, must be made in accordance with the provisions of DOE M 470.4-1, *Safeguards and Security Program Planning and Management* dated 8-26-05.

6. <u>DEFINITIONS</u>. Terms commonly used in the program are defined in DOE M 470.4-7, *Safeguards and Security Program References*, dated 8-26-05.

7. <u>REFERENCES</u>.

    a.   References commonly used in the S&S Program are located in DOE M 470.4-7.

    b.   Title XXXII of Public Law (P.L.) 106-65, National Nuclear Security Administration Act, as amended, which established a separately organized agency within the DOE.

8. <u>IMPLEMENTATION</u>. Requirements that cannot be implemented within 6 months of the effective date of this Manual or within existing resources must be documented by the cognizant security authority and submitted to the relevant program officers; the Under

Secretary for Energy; the Under Secretary for Science; or the Under Secretary for Nuclear Security/Administrator, NNSA; and the Office of Security Policy, Office of Health, Safety and Security. The documentation must include timelines and resources needed to fully implement this Manual. The documentation must also include a description of the vulnerabilities and impacts created by delayed implementation of the requirements.

9.   <u>CONTACT</u>. Questions concerning this Manual should be directed to the Office of Security Policy, Office of Health, Safety and Security, at 301-903-6209.

BY ORDER OF THE SECRETARY OF ENERGY:

 DANIEL B. PONEMAN
Deputy Secretary

TABLE OF CONTENTS

Part 1. PHYSICAL PROTECTION.. i

Chapter I. PROTECTION PLANNING I-1

Chapter II. SECURITY AREAS... II-1

Chapter III. POSTING NOTICES III-1

Chapter IV. LOCKS AND KEYS IV-1

Chapter V. MAINTENANCE.. V-1

Chapter VI. BARRIERS VI-1

Chapter VII. COMMUNICATIONS, ELECTRICAL POWER AND LIGHTING VII-1

Chapter VIII. SECURE STORAGE VIII-1

Chapter IX. INTRUSION DETECTION AND ASSESSMENT SYSTEMS IX-1

Chapter X. ENTRY/EXIT SCREENING X-1

CHAPTER A-I. PROTECTION OF CATEGORY III AND IV SPECIAL NUCLEAR
    MATERIAL A-I-1

CHAPTER A-II. ALARM MANAGEMENT AND CONTROL SYSTEM....................... A-II-1

CHAPTER A-III. INTRUSION DETECTION AND ASSESSMENT SYSTEMS A-III-1

CHAPTER A-IV. COMMUNICATIONS..A-IV-1

CHAPTER A-V. PROTECTION DURING TRANSPORTATION A-V-1

CHAPTER B-I. PROTECTION OF NUCLEAR WEAPONS, COMPONENTS, AND
    CATEGORY I AND II SPECIAL NUCLEAR MATERIAL.......................................B-I-1

CHAPTER B-II. ALARM MANAGEMENT AND CONTROL SYSTEM B-II-1

CHAPTER B-III. COMMUNICATIONS, ELECTRICAL POWER, AND LIGHTING B-III-1

CHAPTER B-IV. INTRUSION DETECTION AND ASSESSMENT SYSTEMS..............B-IV-1

CHAPTER B-V. ACCESS CONTROLS AND ENTRY/EXIT INSPECTIONS B-V-1

CHAPTER B-VI. SECURE STORAGE B-VI-1

CHAPTER B-VII. PROTECTIVE FORCE POSTS B-VII-1

CHAPTER B-VIII. BARRIERS B-VIII-1

CHAPTER B-IX. PROTECTION DURING TRANSPORTATION B-IX-1

APPENDIX C. SAFEGUARDS AND SECURITY ALARM MANAGEMENT AND
    CONTROL SYSTEMS (SAMACS) C-1

ATTACHMENT 1. CONTRACTOR REQUIREMENTS DOCUMENT

ATTACHMENT 2. DOE SECURITY BADGE PROGRAM

CHAPTER I. PROTECTION PLANNING

1.   <u>GENERAL REQUIREMENTS</u>. This Manual establishes requirements for the physical
      protection of all Departmental interests including Departmental property and national
      S&S interests under DOE purview. Interests requiring protection range from Government
      facilities, buildings, property and employees, to national security interests such as
      classified information, SNM and nuclear weapons. Radiological, chemical, or biological
      sabotage targets must be provided protection as determined by vulnerability analysis.
      Select biological agents and toxins are also considered DOE interests. Protection of these
      select biological agents and toxins are governed by Title 7 Code of Federal Regulations
      (CFR) Part 331, *Possession, Use, and Transfer of Select Agents and Toxins*; 9 CFR Part
      121, *Possession, Use, and Transfer of Select Agents and Toxins*; 9 CFR Part 122,
      Organisms and Vectors; and 42 CFR Part 73, *Select Agents and Toxins*. Protection of
      chemical facilities/activities which are considered to present a high risk are governed by
      Title 6 CFR Part 27, *Chemical Facility Anti-Terrorism Standards; Final Rule.*

      a.   Depending on the interest, protection may be required based on best business
            practices, economic rationale, national security objectives or other rationale.

      b.   DOE line management must consider the various Departmental interests and their
            attractiveness to theft, diversion or sabotage and develop protection requirements
            using graded protection fundamentals.

      c.   Physical protection strategies must be developed, documented, and implemented
            consistent with the Graded Security Protection (GSP), formerly the Design Basis
            Threat Policy, and National policy to protect against radiological, chemical, or
            biological sabotage (see DOE O 470.3B, *Graded Security Protection Policy*).

2.   <u>PLANNING</u>. The implementation of graded physical protection programs required by
      this Manual must be systematically planned, executed, evaluated, and documented as
      described by a site security plan (see DOE M 470.4-1).

      a.   Physical protection programs must be based on the most recent GSP information
            and used in conjunction with local threat guidance. The GSP applies to all DOE
            facilities including those that do not possess classified matter or SNM (see
            DOE O 470.3B).

      b.   Departmental interests must be protected from malevolent acts such as theft,
            diversion, and sabotage and events such as natural disasters and civil disorder by
            considering site and regional threats, protection planning strategies, and
            protection measures.

      c.   SNM must be protected at the higher level when roll-up to a higher category can
            occur within a single security area unless the facility has conducted an analysis
            that determined roll-up was not credible (see DOE M 470.4-6 Chg 1 and
            DOE M 470.4-7).

d.   Sites upgrading security measures must consider the benefits provided using security technology by conducting life-cycle cost-benefit analyses comparing the effectiveness of security technology to traditional manpower-based methodologies. However, at Category I and Category II facilities various manpower alternatives to include security technologies must be used to allow protective force personnel to concentrate on the primary mission of protecting nuclear weapons, SNM, and designated high-value targets.

3.   PERFORMANCE ASSURANCE. Physical protection systems, including components, must be performance tested to ensure overall system effectiveness. The effectiveness of physical protection systems and programs must be determined through performance testing at a frequency determined by the cognizant security authority and in accordance with the Performance Assurance Program. A program of scheduled testing and maintenance must be implemented to ensure an effective, fully functional security system (see DOE M 470.4-1).

4.   PHYSICAL PROTECTION SURVEILLANCE EQUIPMENT. If physical protection surveillance equipment is to be used to support the facility's physical protection strategy, it must be identified and its physical protection application must be described in the site security plan. Procedures must be developed to prohibit misuse of physical protection surveillance equipment (e.g., video assessment and audio communication/recording equipment).

CHAPTER II. SECURITY AREAS

1. <u>GENERAL REQUIREMENTS</u>. Security areas are established to provide protection to a wide array of S&S interests under the Department's purview, to include nuclear weapons, SNM, classified information, buildings, facilities, Government property, employees and other interests. The security areas described in this Chapter address a graded approach for the protection of S&S interests.

2. <u>GENERAL ACCESS AREAS (GAAs)</u>. GAAs may be established to allow access to certain areas with minimum security requirements as determined by the cognizant security authority.

    a. <u>General Requirements</u>. These designated areas are accessible to all personnel including the public. DOE line management should establish security requirements for those areas designated as a GAA.

    b. <u>Posting of General Access Areas</u>. The designated GAA security requirements must be posted to inform all personnel, including the public, that entry into these areas subjects them to the security requirements. The posting should list the security conditions (see 41 CFR Part 102-74 Subpart C).

3. <u>PROPERTY PROTECTION AREAS (PPAs)</u>. PPAs are security areas that are established to protect employees and Government buildings, facilities and property.

    a. <u>General Requirements</u>. The requirements for PPAs must be configured to protect Government-owned property and equipment against damage, destruction, or theft and must provide a means to control public access. Protection may include physical barriers, access control systems, biometric systems, protective personnel or persons assigned administrative or other authorized security duties, intrusion detection systems, locks and keys, etc. The cognizant security authority must designate, describe, and document PPA protection measures within their SSP.

    b. <u>Signs. Signs prohibiting Trespassing</u>. Warning signs and/or notices must be posted around the perimeter and at entrances to a PPA. (see Chapter III). For General Services Administration (GSA) leased buildings and offices, GSA guidance implementing 41 CFR Part 102-74.365 describes the posting requirements.

        (1) Signs listing prohibited articles must be posted at PPA entrances. Additional prohibited and controlled article signs may be posted at inner security areas [Limited Area (LA), Exclusion Area (EA), Protected Area (PA) and/or Material Access Area (MAA)] as determined by the cognizant security authority. The listing of controlled articles is to be prepared by the sites.

(2)   Warning signs and/or notices must be posted at entrances to areas under electronic surveillance advising that physical protection surveillance equipment is in operation.

c.   Access Control. Access controls must be implemented to protect employees, property, and facilities. Security requirements for personnel and vehicles entering the PPA must be established by the cognizant security authority. Procedures for the processing of visitors, including foreign nationals must be approved by the cognizant security authority and documented in the SSP (see Attachment 2, DOE M 470.4-2A).

d.   Parking Areas. If parking areas are near security areas and could interfere with intrusion detection sensor fields, clear zones, protective force (PF) operations, or pose a threat to target areas, these parking issues must be addressed in the SSP.

(1)   Parking areas must not impact security equipment, security operations or be located in manner that degrades protection of Departmental interests.

(2)   Vehicle bomb threats must be considered in determining the location of vehicle parking areas. For all new construction, parking areas should be located at a pre-determined distance from buildings to minimize a vehicle bomb threat. The set-back distance must be determined by using the site GSP and vulnerability assessment.

e.   Inspection Program. An inspection program is to deter prohibited and controlled articles being brought into PPA facilities. All personnel, vehicles, packages, and hand-carried articles are subject to inspection before entry into a security area. Likewise, such programs must ensure that S&S interests are not removed. If implemented, the inspection program must be established by the cognizant security authority and documented in the SSP.

f.   Intrusion Detection. If used, security requirements for intrusion detection, including long range detection technologies, for the PPA must be established by the cognizant security authority.

g.   Visitor Processing. Site specific requirements and procedures for receiving visitors must be developed and approved by the cognizant security authority. For Exclusion Areas, Protected Areas, and Material Access Areas, the procedures must provide for recording the following visitor information for paper entries: printed full name and signature, organization represented, citizenship, person to be visited, purpose of visit, escort name, time of entry and exit. For electronic log entries when using automatic access control systems, full name, agency or organization represented, citizenship; purpose of the visit, clearance level, if validated, escort's name, and time of entry.

(1)   Information from visitor logs must be retained in accordance with local records management procedures.

(2)   Paper visitor logs must plainly reflect the penalty of false personation and representation. Sites using electronic visitor processing must post signs reflecting the penalty for false impersonation and representation.

       (a)   Laws regarding the penalty for false personating are stated in 18 U.S.C. Part 1, Section 911.

       (b)   Laws regarding fraud and false statements are stated in 18 U.S.C. Part 1, Section 1001.

4.   <u>LIMITED AREAS (LAs)</u>. LAs are security areas designated for the protection of classified matter and Category III and higher quantities of special nuclear material (SNM) and to serve as a concentric layer of protection. Specific protection requirements applicable to Category III quantities of SNM are provided in Appendix A.

   a.   <u>General Requirements</u>. LA boundaries are defined by physical barriers encompassing the designated space and access controls to ensure that only authorized personnel are allowed to enter the LA.

   b.   <u>Access Control</u>. The identity and clearance level of each person seeking entry to an LA must be validated by PF, or other appropriately authorized personnel, or by an automated system and documented in the SSP.

      (1)   If automated access control equipment is used, a DOE security badge must be used to access the LA.

      (2)   Entry control points for vehicle and pedestrian access to LA must provide the same level of protection as that provided at all other points along the security perimeter.

      (3)   Exits from LAs must satisfy life safety requirements of National Fire Protection Association (NFPA) 101, *Safety to Life from Fire in Buildings and Structures*. Some exits may be provided for emergency use only.

         (a)   Security area entrances and exits must be equipped with doors, gates, rails, or other movable barriers that direct and control the movement of personnel or vehicles through designated control points.

         (b)   Automated gates must be designed to allow manual operation during power outages or mechanism failures.

    (c)   Site-specific requirements and procedures for receiving visitors must be developed and approved by the cognizant security authority.

    (d)   Information from visitor logs must be retained in accordance with local records management procedures.

c.   <u>Personnel Access</u>. Individuals without a security clearance must be escorted by an authorized person who is to ensure measures are taken to prevent a compromise of classified matter.

    (1)   Escort Ratios. The cognizant security authority must establish escort-to-visitor ratios in a graded manner for each LA or above security area.

    (2)   Escort Responsibilities. Any person permitted to enter a LA or above who does not possess a security clearance at the appropriate level must be escorted at all times by an appropriately cleared and knowledgeable individual trained in local escort procedures.

        (a)   Escorts must ensure measures are taken to prevent compromise of S&S interests.

        (b)   The escort must ensure the visitor has a need-to-know for the security area or the S&S interests.

    (3)   Access Validation. Validations must occur at entry control points of LAs.

        (a)   The identity and security clearance held by each person seeking entry must be validated by appropriately authorized personnel, automated systems, or other means documented in the SSP.

        (b)   Where practicable, PF personnel will not be used to control access to LAs.

    (4)   "Piggybacking." The following requirements must be documented in the SSP if piggybacking into LAs is permitted.

        (a)   Personnel with the appropriate security clearance may vouch for another person with the required security clearance to "piggyback" into an LA.

        (b)   Authorized personnel permitting the entry of another person must inspect the individual's DOE security badge to ensure that it bears a likeness of the individual and that he or she has the proper security clearance identifier on the badge. When PF personnel are not controlling access to the LA, the DOE federal or contractor employee authorized to enter the LA is responsible for ensuring that those accompanying individuals are authorized entry.

(5)   Automated Access Control Systems. Automated access control systems may be used if the following requirements are met.

    (a)   Automated access controls used for access to a LA or above security area must verify that the DOE security badge is valid (i.e., that the badge data read by the system match the data assigned to the badge holder).

    (b)   When remote, unattended, automated access control system entry control points are used for access to LA and above security areas, the barrier must be resistant to bypass. The unattended entry control point should have closed-circuit television system coverage.

    (c)   Automated control system alarms (e.g., annunciation of a door alarm, duress alarm, tamper alarm, or anti-passback indication feature) must be treated as an intrusion alarm for the area being protected.

    (d)   Personnel or other protective measures are required to protect card reader access transactions, displays (e.g., badge-encoded data), and keypad devices. The process of inputting, storing, displaying, or recording verification data must ensure that the data are protected in accordance with the SSP.

    (e)   The system must record all attempts at access to include unsuccessful, unauthorized, and authorized.

    (f)   Door locks opened by badge readers must be designed to relock immediately after the door has closed.

    (g)   Transmission lines that carry security clearance and personal identification or verification data between devices/equipment must be protected in accordance with the SSP.

    (h)   Records reflecting active assignments of DOE security badges, security clearance, and similar system-related records must be maintained. Records of personnel removed from the system must be retained for 1 year, unless a longer period is specified by other requirements. Personal data must be protected in conformance with the Privacy Act, (see 5 U.S.C. 552a).

    (i)   Badge reader boxes, control lines, and junction boxes must have line supervision or tamper indication or be equipped with tamper-resistant devices. Data Gathering Panels/Field processors or multiplexers and other similar equipment must be tamper-alarmed or secured by a means that precludes surreptitious tampering with the equipment.

(j)   Uninterrupted power supply or compensatory measures must be provided at installations where continuous operation is required.

d.   <u>Vehicle Access.</u>

(1)   Approval for non-Government vehicles, which includes privately owned, to access LAs must be documented in the SSP.

(2)   Government-owned or -leased vehicles may be admitted only when on official business and only when operated by properly cleared and authorized drivers.

(3)   The SSP must identify procedures for inspection of, and access by, service and delivery vehicles. Factors to be considered are vehicle identification, identification of owner/operator and provision for various technologies to include vehicle navigation systems, cell phones and back-up cameras.

(4)   All personnel within a vehicle are required to produce DOE security badges when accessing an LA and comply with individual LA procedures.

(5)   When a remote automated access control system is used for vehicle access control, it must verify that the operator or the escort has a valid DOE security badge (e.g., the badge data read by the system must match the data assigned to the badge holder).

e.   <u>Signs</u>. Signs must be posted to convey information on the prohibited and controlled articles; the inspection of vehicles, packages, hand-carried items, and persons entering or exiting the security area; the use of video surveillance equipment; and trespassing (see Title 42 United States Code (U.S.C.) Section 2278a). The decision on the signage and posting rests with the cognizant security authority and the requirements cited in federal statutes and regulations (see Chapter III).

5.   <u>EXCLUSION AREAS (EAs)</u>. EAs are established to protect classified matter where an individual's mere presence may result in access to classified matter.

a.   <u>General Requirements</u>. The boundaries of EAs must be encompassed by physical barriers and be located within the minimum of an LA or receive approval of the cognizant security authority for those EAs not within a minimum of a LA.

b.   <u>Access Control</u>. In addition to the requirements for an LA the following requirements apply to access to an EA.

(1)   Individuals permitted unescorted access must have the appropriate access authorizations and a need-to-know consistent with the classified matter to which they have access by virtue of their presence in the EA.

(2)   Individuals without the appropriate security clearance and need-to-know must be escorted by a knowledgeable individual who must ensure measures are taken to prevent compromise of classified matter.

(3)   Visitor logs must be used for EAs. The requirements cited in paragraph 3.f, above, should be considered when establishing a visitor log process.

c.   Intrusion Detection.

(1)   Unauthorized entry into the EA must be detected.

(2)   When the exclusion area is unoccupied, and classified matter is not secured in a security container, then the EA must at a minimum, meet the requirements of a vault-type room (VTR) or an appropriate level of protection as determined by the cognizant security authority.

6.   SPECIAL DESIGNATED SECURITY AREAS. Other areas with access restrictions include CASs, secondary alarm stations (SASs), Sensitive Compartmented Information Facilities (SCIFs), Special Access Program Facilities (SAPFs), classified conferencing rooms, secure communications centers, and automated information system centers.

a.   Special Access Programs (SAP). The technical requirements for SAPs are identified in DOE M 471.2-3B, *Special Access Program Policies, Responsibilities, and Procedures*, dated 10-29-07, and DOE M 470.4-1.

b.   Alarm Stations. Security system requirements are described in Appendix A.

c.   Sensitive Compartmented Information Facilities. DOE follows the requirements in Director of Central Intelligence Directive (DCID) 6/9 and DCID Manual 6/9 dated 11-18-02, DOE O 5639.8A, *Security of Foreign Intelligence Information and Sensitive Compartmented Information Facilities*, dated 7-23-93, and DOE *Sensitive Compartmented Information Facility Procedural Guide* for the construction and accreditation of SCIFs.

d.   Other Designated Security Alarm Stations. If response to an alarm activity by LLEA/security personnel is permitted, then the alarm company/service must meet the specifications contained in Underwriters Laboratories (UL) Standard 827, *Standard for Central-Station Alarm Services.*

e.   Classified Conferencing Areas, Secure Communications Centers and Automated Information System Centers. (For the purpose of this requirement, areas, centers, and facilities are the locations where a specific activity takes place).

    (1)   Classified information is to be protected in conformance with DOE Information Security policy (see DOE M 470.4-4A).

    (2)   Separate access controls and barriers must be established to restrict access to only persons employed in secure communication and automated information centers handling classified information or otherwise requiring access to perform their official duties.

    (3)   Security clearances consistent with the highest level and category of classified information handled are required for all persons assigned to or having unescorted access to the above centers. A list of persons who have authorized access must be maintained within the center, and a record must be maintained of all visitors entering the facility.

    (4)   The design of automated information system centers and remote interrogation points that process classified information must consider the following:

        (a)   Establishment of a control zone consisting of the area above, below, and around equipment and distribution systems that have been inspected and are to be kept under physical and technical control to prevent unauthorized access, is required.

        (b)   Separate access controls and barriers. When contained within a larger designated security area, automated information system centers and remote interrogation points used to process classified information must have separate access controls and barriers.

    (5)   The selection of conferencing facilities for the conduct of classified meetings, and teleconferencing must conform to Information Security policy (see DOE M 470.4-4A).

7.   <u>PROHIBITED AND CONTROLLED ARTICLES</u>. Authorization for prohibited articles to be used for official Government business must be documented in a SSP. The articles listed below will not be permitted onto DOE property without appropriate authorization.

    a.   <u>Prohibited Articles</u>. Prohibited articles include items such as:

        (1)   explosives,

        (2)   dangerous weapons,

        (3)   instruments or material likely to produce substantial injury to persons or damage to persons or property,

        (4)   controlled substances (e.g., illegal drugs and associated paraphernalia but not prescription medicine), and

(5)   other items prohibited by law. Specific information covering prohibited items may be found under the provisions of 10 CFR Part 860 and 41 CFR Part 102-74 Subpart C.

b.   <u>Controlled Articles</u>.

    (1)   Controlled articles such as portable electronic devices, both Government and personally owned, capable of recording information or transmitting data (e.g., audio, video, radio frequency, infrared, and/or data link electronic equipment) are not permitted in limited areas (LAs), exclusion areas (EAs) protected areas (PAs), and material access areas (MAAs), without prior approval. The approval process must be documented in the SSP. NOTE: Government-owned computer systems which are part of the day-to-day operations are exempt from the requirement. The cognizant security authority must specify the equipment to be exempted from the approval process.

    (2)   Sites are to develop procedures to account for, control, and limit all controlled articles entering specified security areas. These procedures must be approved by the cognizant security authority.

        (a)   For application to Special Access Program Facilities (SAPFs), Sensitive Compartmented Information Facilities (SCIFs), etc., the Director Central Intelligence Directive (DCID) 6/9 and DCID manual, *Physical Security Standards for Sensitive Compartmented Information Facilities*, program guidance must be implemented.

                For SAPFs, the programmatic policy addressing Controlled Articles, would be issued by the Special Access Program Administrator (see DOE M 471.2-3B, *Special Access Program Polices, Responsibilities, and Procedures*).

        (b)   Office of Secure Transportation Federal Agents, DOE protective personnel, and other Federal agents and Local Law Enforcement Officials with jurisdiction, whose duties routinely require the carrying and operation of controlled articles, are exempt from this requirement unless a nuclear safety reason exists to prohibit certain communication devices, e.g., cellular telephones, transceiver-radios and other electronic radiating/emitting devices. If such a prohibition exists, it is to be documented in specific agreements between the site and Federal agency.

CHAPTER III. POSTING NOTICES

1. <u>GENERAL REQUIREMENTS</u>. Signs must be posted at facilities, installations, and real property based on the need to implement Federal statutes protecting against degradation of S&S interests.

2. <u>TRESPASSING</u>. DOE property must be posted according to statutes, regulations, and the administrative requirements for posting specified in this Manual.

    a. <u>Statutory and Regulatory Provisions</u>.

        (1) Section 229 of the Atomic Energy Act of 1954 (42 U.S.C. 2278a) as implemented by 10 CFR 860, prohibits unauthorized entry and unauthorized carrying, transporting, or otherwise introducing or causing to be introduced any dangerous explosives, or other dangerous instrument or matter likely to produce substantial injury to persons or damage to property into or upon any facility, installation, or real property subject to the jurisdiction, administration, or in the custody of DOE. The statute provides for posting the regulations and penalties for violations.

        (2) Section 662 of the DOE Organization Act (42 U.S.C. 7270b), as implemented by 10 CFR 1048, prohibits unauthorized entry upon and unauthorized carrying, transporting, or otherwise introducing or causing to be introduced, any dangerous instrument or material likely to produce substantial injury to persons or damage to property into or onto the Strategic Petroleum Reserve, its storage or related facilities, or real property subject to the jurisdiction, administration, or custody of DOE. The statute provides for posting the regulations and penalties for violations.

        (3) Public Law 566, 80th Congress of June 1, 1948 (Title 40, U.S. Code 318); and the Federal Property and Administrative Services Act of 1949 (title 63, United States Statutes at Large, 377 as amended) provide the rules and regulations governing public buildings and grounds under the charge and control of the GSA. 41 CFR 102-74.365 Subpart C governs entry to public buildings and grounds under the charge and control of the GSA.

        (4) Signs prohibiting trespassing must be posted around the perimeter and at each entrance to a security area except when one security area is within a larger, posted security area. The distance between signage is to be determined by the cognizant security authority.

    b. <u>Posting Proposals</u>. Requirements for the administration of posting proposals are as follows:

(1)   Conditions. Proposals for the posting of facilities, installations, or real property, or amendment to or revocation of a previous proposal must be submitted when one of the following occurs.

(a)   The property is owned by or contracted to the United States for DOE use.

(b)   The property requires protection under the Atomic Energy Act of 1954 and/or of the DOE Organization Act.

(c)   A previous notice needs to be amended or revoked.

(2)   Contents.

(a)   Each posting proposal must include the name and specific location of the installation, facility, or real property to be covered and the boundary coordinates. If boundary coordinates are not available, the proposal must include a description that will furnish reasonable notice of the area to be covered, which may be an entire area or any portion thereof that can be physically delineated by the posting indicated in paragraph 2c below.

(b)   Each proposal for amendment or revocation must identify the property involved, state clearly the action to be taken (i.e., change in property description, correction, or revocation), and contain a new or revised property description, if required.

c.   Posting Requirements.

(1)   Upon approval by the Office of Health, Safety and Security, with concurrence by the Office of General Counsel, a notice designating the facility, installation, or real property subject to the jurisdiction, administration, or in the custody of DOE must be published in the *Federal Register*. The notice is effective upon publication, providing the notices stating the pertinent prohibitions and penalties are posted (see 10 CFR 860.7).

(2)   Property approved by the Office of Health, Safety and Security must be posted at entrances and at such intervals along the perimeter of the property to ensure notification of persons about to enter. Signs must measure at least 11 by 14 inches (28 x 36 centimeters).

(3)   The signs should be configured with a white or yellow background and black lettering. Signs that notify of the use of deadly force should use a white background with red lettering for the words "WARNING USE OF DEADLY FORCE AUTHORIZED." The remaining words should be in black.

(4)   Placement of signs on fences must not interfere with the function of fence-mounted intrusion detection systems (IDS). If the signage interferes with the IDS or closed-circuit television coverage, it could be mounted on posts outside the fenced area. NOTE: The signage should be mounted so that it is easily discernable, midway between fence posts, at approximately 40-50 foot (12.1-15.1 meter) intervals.

d.   <u>Notification to the Federal Bureau of Investigation</u>. Notification, by the program office exercising jurisdiction over the site/facility, of the date of posting, relocation, removal of posting, or other change, and the identity of the property involved must be furnished to the applicable office of the Federal Bureau of Investigation exercising investigative responsibility over the property.

CHAPTER IV. LOCKS AND KEYS

1. <u>GENERAL REQUIREMENTS</u>. A program to protect and manage locks and keys must be established by the cognizant security authority. The lock and key program must be applied in a graded manner based on the S&S interests being protected, identified threat, existing barriers, and other protection measures afforded these interests. Security keys include mechanical keys, key cards, and access codes. Security keys do not include administrative or privacy lock keys to factory-installed file cabinet locks, desk locks, toolboxes, etc. Access codes must be protected from compromise.

2. <u>CATEGORIES</u>. Security keys and locks are divided into four levels, Levels I through IV. These levels are based on the S&S interest being protected and upon a site analysis. Non-security locks and keys are considered Administrative. The cognizant security authority must determine the appropriate level for application to the site. Facilities that do not possess nuclear weapons, weapons components, SNM, classified matter, and high-value government property should follow the requirements established for Level III and Level IV locks and keys.

    a. Level I. Security locations such as vaults, vault-type rooms, material access areas which store nuclear weapons and Category I and Category II that roll-up to a Category I quantity of SNM, and sensitive compartmented information facilities where Top Secret and/or Secret documents are stored require Level I security locks and keys.

    b. Level II. Building doors, entry control points, gates in PAs, fences, doors or other barriers or containers protecting Category II and Category III SNM and Confidential classified matter must be protected by locks and keys categorized as Level II.

    c. Level III. Buildings, gates in fences, cargo containers, and storage areas protecting Category IV SNM, and government property whose loss would adversely impact security and/or site/facility operations must be protected by locks and keys categorized as Level III.

    d. Level IV. Buildings where no classified matter or SNM is in use or stored should be protected by locks and keys categorized as Level IV.

    e. Administrative Keys. Desk, office, supply cabinets and vehicle keys are not considered security keys and have no control and accountability requirements based on the cognizant security authorities guidance. Keys to certain vehicle identified in the sites vulnerability analysis as a particular security concern will require added protection.

3.   <u>LOCK AND KEY STANDARDS</u>.

    a.   Key locksets must meet American National Standards Institute (ANSI) Standard A156.2-1996, Grade 1, Bored and Preassembled Locks and Latches, or ANSI A156.13-1996, Grade 1, Mortise Locksets.

    b.   Locks used in the protection of classified matter and Categories I and II SNM (e.g., security containers, safes, vaults) must meet Federal Specification FF-L-2740A, Locks, Combination.

    c.   All security locks securing containers, vaults, and vault-type rooms placed into service after July 14, 1994 must have a lock that meets Federal Specification FF-L-2740A, Locks, Combination.

    d.   Combination padlocks must meet Federal Specification FF-P-110, Padlock, Changeable Combination, and standards cited in 41 CFR Part 101, Federal Property Management Regulations. These padlocks may be used with the lock bars securing metal filing cabinets. NOTE: These padlocks conform to the standards set forth in National Security Council Directive governing the classification, downgrading, declassification and safeguarding of national security information.

    e.   Security key padlocks must meet the following specifications:

        (1)   High-security, shrouded-shackle, key-operated padlocks must meet standards in Military Specification MIL-DTL-43607H, *Padlock, Key Operated, High Security, Shrouded Shackle*. High-security padlocks are approved to secure Category I and II SNM and Top Secret and/or Secret matter and are identified as a Level I.

        (2)   Low-security, regular (open-shackle, key-operated padlocks) must meet the classes and standards in Commercial Item Description A-A-59486 and A-A-59487. The cognizant security authority must determine low-security padlock usage based upon the site analysis conducted on the security interest being protected.

        (3)   Lock bars used to secure file cabinets containing classified information must be 1¼ inches (31.75 millimeters) by 3/16 inch (4.76 millimeters) or equivalent in cross section and constructed of rigid metal material. NOTE: Securing file cabinets with locking bars will not be acceptable after October 1, 2012.

        (4)   Hasps and yokes on containers storing classified matter must be constructed of steel material, be at least ¼ inch (6.35 millimeters) in diameter or equivalent cross section, and be secured to the container by welding, or riveting, to preclude removal.

(5)   General field service padlock is a heavy-duty, exposed shackle lock that meets Federal Specification FF-P-2827. The key-operated padlock is designed for non-high security application where there is exposure to grit and corrosive or freezing environments. The cognizant security authority must determine general field service padlock usage based on a site analysis conducted on the security interest being protected.

f.   Panic hardware or emergency exit mechanisms used on emergency doors located in security areas must be operable only from inside the perimeter and must meet all applicable Life Safety Codes (see DOE M 470.4-7).

g.   Keys, key blanks, and key cutting codes must be protected in a graded fashion. Consideration must be given to the S&S interest being protected, the identified threat, existing barriers, and other protection measures afforded to the interest. Locks and keys must be categorized according to the interest being protected. An inventory and accountability system must be implemented.

h.   Security key stock must be stored in a manner to prevent loss, theft, or unauthorized use. (Security keys are devices that can open a lock and can include mechanical keys, key cards, access codes, and potentially other non-standard types of devices. Security keys do not include administrative or privacy lock keys to factory installed file cabinet locks, desk locks, toolboxes, etc.). Access codes that may open a lock that controls access to a security interest must be protected from compromise. Personnel responsible for the control and issuance of locking systems and/or security keys, including key cards (when used in place of mechanical keys), must maintain a security clearance commensurate with that required for access to the interest to which the keys provide direct access.

(1)   The organization responsible for the pinning and cutting of Levels I, II, and III security locks and keys must report to the cognizant security authority.

(2)   The pinning and cutting of Levels I, II, and III security locks and keys must be done within an LA or have equivalent type protection measures.

(3)   The use and protection strategy for grand master, master, sub-master, and control keys, etc., must be considered, analyzed and documented in the SSP. Master keys will not be used in the-protection of Category I SNM.

4.   <u>INVENTORY</u>. An inventory system must be implemented to ensure the accountability of Levels I, II, and III security locks, keys, key rings, key ways, and pinned cores and documented in the SSP. A hands-on inventory must be conducted for all keys and padlocks both in use and in storage, as specified below. NOTE: The requirements for inventorying of locks do not apply to the XO series of combination locks installed on security containers and vaults/vault-type-rooms. Each accountable key and key core, including key cards (when used in place of mechanical keys), must have an affixed unique and permanent identifying number.

a. Fabrication, issuance, return, and destruction of Levels I, II, and III security locks and keys must be documented.

   (1) Duplicate and replacement keys must not have the same key number assigned as the key being replaced or duplicated.

   (2) Grand master security keys must be kept to an operational minimum and protected at the highest level of S&S interest being protected. NOTE: Grand master security keys include a system wherein a series of locks are keyed alike.

   (3) The inventory record must identify the specific duplicate and replacement keys. If replaced, the disposition of the key being replaced must be recorded.

   (4) Include in inventory records locks, keys in possession of key holders, issuance stock, and keys assigned to key rings/key cabinets. The inventory record should include the list of the locations of locks that each key will open.

   (5) Document each person issued a Level I security lock and key and the individual who issued the locks and key.

   (6) Document the locations of the locks and keys.

b. There must be a 100 percent inventory of all Level I security locks and keys.

   (1) Support the 100 percent inventory of Level I security locks and keys that must be performed on a semi-annual basis by the responsible organization.

   (2) An annual inventory must be conducted of locks in storage and all keys in storage or use.

   (3) Provide support in inventorying of Level I security keys not assigned to an individual (e.g., key rings, key cabinets, and keys issued on a temporary basis) that must be performed daily. Accountability of tamper indicating key rings is sufficient when used.

c. Key rings for Level I and II must have a unique identifying number placed on the ring.

d. Support a 100 percent inventory of all Levels II and III locks and keys on an annual basis by the responsible organization.

e. When a Level I security key is unaccounted for, immediate notification must be made to the cognizant security authority, compensatory measures must be immediately initiated, and an incident of security concern inquiry must be completed. If the key cannot be located within 24 hours, the affected lock must be changed.

f.   Level IV locks and keys have no inventory requirement.

g.   Sites must have documented procedures for key turn-in when personnel or programs are terminating or when an individual no longer has a need for the key.

5.   LEVEL I SECURITY KEYS AND LOCKS.

a.   Level I keys and locks control access to nuclear weapons, weapons components, Category I quantities of SNM, Category II quantities if SNM that credibly roll-up to a Category I quantity, certain high-value government property, and Secret or higher classified matter must be protected by locks and keys categorized as Level I. Level I key blanks must be restricted/proprietary; specifically, the blank must be unique to the site (e.g., it does not use a commercially available master key blank).

b.   Once they are put in service inside a PA, Level I security locks and keys must not leave the PA without authorization as described in the SSP. Any key that leaves the PA without authorization shall be considered unaccounted for and reported as lost. When not in use for the protection of the above interests (e.g., locksmith service work) the assembled Level I security locks or cores and Level I security keys must remain under the direct control of an authorized person or must be stored in a General Services Administration (GSA)-approved security container or a vault-type room (or other location as identified in the SSP with equivalent protection). Access to the Level I security locks and keys must be controlled and limited to authorized personnel.

c.   Sites must conduct and document an assessment of duties for possible enrollment of locksmith personnel into the DOE Human Reliability Program (10 CFR 712).

d.   Any installation, replacement, or maintenance activities associated with Level I security locks must be documented to include the name of a person who performed the activity.

e.   The number of Level I keys must be kept to an operational minimum.

f.   Level I keys must be on a separate key ring from all other levels of keys.

g.   All parts of broken Level I security keys should be recovered. If the functional part of the key (the blade) is lost or not retrievable, it must be reported as a lost/missing key as required by Impact Measurement Index (IMI) categorization cited in Section N, DOE M 470.4-1.

h.   Obsolete, damaged, or inoperative Level I keys must be destroyed in a manner authorized by the cognizant security authority and the destruction recorded.

i. In order for corrective actions to be taken quickly after an incident involving the loss, theft, or destruction of a Level I lock or key, a risk assessment and compensatory measures must be pre-established and documented.

6. <u>LEVEL II SECURITY KEYS AND LOCKS</u>.

a. Level II security locks and keys must be used to control access to Category II and Category III SNM as well as Confidential classified matter. These typically are used for building doors, entry control points, gates in PA fences, LA doors or other barriers or containers. When not in use for the protection of the above interests (e.g., locksmith service work) the Assembled Level II security locks or cores and Level II security keys must remain under the direct control of an authorized person or must be stored in a GSA-approved security container or a vault-type room (or other location as identified in the SSP with equivalent protection). Access to the Level II security locks and keys must be controlled and limited to authorized personnel.

b. The number of Level II keys must be kept to an operational minimum.

c. Level II locks and keys once put into service must not leave the site without cognizant security authority approval.

d. All parts of broken Level II security keys should be recovered; if the functional part of the key (the blade) is lost or not retrievable, it must be reported as a lost/missing key.

e. Obsolete, damaged, or inoperative Level II keys must be destroyed in a manner authorized by the cognizant security authority and such destruction recorded.

f. Incidents involving Level II keys and locks must be reported. (see IMI categorization cited in DOE M 470.4-1).

7. <u>LEVEL III SECURITY KEYS AND LOCKS</u>.

a. Level III security locks and keys control access to Category IV SNM and Government property and are typically associated with buildings, gates in fences, cargo containers, and storage areas.

b. All parts of broken Level III security keys must be recovered; if the functional part of the key (the blade) is lost or not retrievable, it must be reported to the cognizant security authority.

c. Obsolete, damaged, or inoperative Level III keys must be destroyed in a manner authorized by the cognizant security authority and such destruction recorded.

d. Site-specific procedures must be developed for the control of Level III security locks and keys and be approved by the cognizant security authority.

e.   If a Level III lock or key is discovered to be missing or tampered with, the incident must be reported to DOE Headquarters (see DOE M 470.4-1), unless the cognizant security authority re-evaluates the IMI categorization level.

8.   <u>LEVEL IV SECURITY KEYS AND LOCKS</u>. Level IV locks and keys are typically used for buildings or offices where there is no open storage of classified matter and no classified matter in use. Desk, office and vehicle keys are considered administrative and have no control and accountability requirements.

CHAPTER V. MAINTENANCE

1. <u>GENERAL REQUIREMENTS</u>. Security-related subsystems and components must be maintained in operable condition. A regularly scheduled testing and maintenance program must be established and documented.

2. <u>CORRECTIVE MAINTENANCE</u>. Corrective maintenance must be performed on site-determined critical and non-critical system elements.

    a. <u>Compensatory Measures</u>. Compensatory measures must be implemented immediately when any part of a critical system element protecting vital equipment, Top Secret matter, SNM, SCI or SAP interests is out of service. Compensatory measures must be continued until maintenance is complete and the system element is back in service.<u>Corrective Maintenance within 24 Hours</u>. Corrective maintenance must be initiated within 24 hours of receiving a report that there has been a malfunction of a site-determined critical system element protecting vital equipment, Top Secret matter, SCI or SAP interests.

    c. <u>Corrective Maintenance within 72 Hours</u>. Corrective maintenance must be initiated within 72 hours of detection of a malfunction for all other system elements protecting, vital equipment, Top Secret matter SCI or SAP interest.

    d. <u>Other Corrective Maintenance</u>. Corrective maintenance procedures for systems protecting Secret or Confidential matter must be approved by the cognizant security authority and prescribed in site operation procedures.

    e. <u>Non-Critical System Maintenance</u>. For non-critical system elements, the cognizant security authority must approve compensatory measure implementation procedures.

3. <u>PREVENTIVE MAINTENANCE</u>. Preventive maintenance must be performed on S&S-related subsystems and components in accordance with manufacturers' specifications and/or local procedures. Remote maintenance of active systems shall not be performed by uncleared personnel.

4. <u>MAINTENANCE PERSONNEL SECURITY CLEARANCES</u>. Personnel who test, maintain, or service critical system elements must have security clearances consistent with the S&S interest being protected.

    a. Security clearances are not required when testing and maintenance are performed as bench services away from the security area.

    b. Systems or critical system elements bench-tested or maintained away from the security area by personnel without the appropriate security clearances must be inspected and operationally tested by qualified and cleared personnel before being returned to service.

c.   Personnel who test, maintain, or service non-critical system elements must have security clearances consistent with the S&S interest being protected as determined by the cognizant security authority.

5.   <u>TESTING AND MAINTENANCE OF SCREENING EQUIPMENT</u>. Screening equipment can include explosive detectors, metal detectors, and x-ray systems and must be capable of detecting prohibited and controlled articles are detected before being permitted into Department of Energy facilities.

   a.   The following should be used as standard test weapons for metal detectors or the site must implement the performance testing procedures and test objects cited in Sections 5.1, 5.2 and the portion of 5.3 of NIJ Standard 0601.02, Law Enforcement and Corrections Standards and Testing Program, relating to non-ferromagnetic stainless steel knives:

      (1)   steel and aluminum alloy .25 caliber automatic pistol manufactured in Italy by Armi Tanfoglio Giuseppe, sold in the United States by Excam as Model GT27B and by F.I.E. as the Titan (weight: about 343 grams); or

      (2)   aluminum, model 7, .380 caliber Derringer manufactured by American Derringer Corporation (weight: about 200 grams); and

      (3)   stainless steel 0.22 caliber long rifle mini-revolver, manufactured by North American Arms (weight: about 129 grams).

   b.   X-ray machines may be used to supplement metal detectors and protective personnel hand searches for prohibited and controlled articles.

      (1)   X-ray machines must provide a discernable image of prohibited and controlled articles.

      (2)   X-ray machines must image an unobstructed (discernable) set of wires and other objects as described in American Society for Testing and Materials (ASTM) standard for test objects (see ASTM Standard F792-01e2, Standard Practice for Evaluating the Imaging Performance of Security X-ray Systems).

6.   <u>RECORD KEEPING</u>.

   a.   Record of the failure and repair of all communication equipment must be maintained so that type of failure, unit serial number, and equipment type can be compiled.

   b.   Testing and maintenance records must be retained in accordance with the requirements of approved records management procedures.

CHAPTER VI. BARRIERS

1. <u>GENERAL REQUIREMENTS</u>. Physical barriers serve as the physical demarcation of the security area. Barriers such as fences, walls, and doors or activated barriers must be used to deter and delay unauthorized access. At a minimum, an analysis is required of high consequence security areas to determine the protection measures against Vehicle Borne Improvised Explosive Devices (VBIED). Barriers may be used to support the prevention of stand-off-attacks.

    a. Barriers must be used to direct the flow of personnel and vehicular traffic through designated entry control points to permit efficient operation of access controls and entry point inspections and to provide the ability to identify and engage adversaries along all feasible pathways.

    b. Entry control points must be designed to provide a barrier resistant to bypass.

    c. Permanent barriers must be used to enclose security areas, except during construction or temporary activities, when temporary barriers may be erected.

    d. Barriers such as fences, walls, and doors may be used to identify the boundary of the property protection area and to provide protection. Barriers must be capable of controlling, impeding, or denying access to a security area.

    e. Fences used should be installed no closer than 20 feet (6 meters) from the building or S&S interest being protected.

2. <u>PENETRATION OF SECURITY AREA BARRIERS</u>. Penetration of security area barrier requirements includes the following.

    a. Elevators that penetrate a security area barrier must be provided with an access control system that is equivalent to the access control requirements for the security area being penetrated.

    b. Utility corridors that penetrate security area barriers must provide the same degree of penetration resistance as the barriers they penetrate.

    c. Objects that intruders could use to scale or bridge barriers and enter security areas must be removed or secured to prevent their unauthorized use.

    d. If a security area configuration is altered, barriers must be erected (e.g., during construction or temporary activities), and at a minimum, a risk assessment must be conducted to validate equivalent protection measures.

    e. The barrier design must consider proximity to buildings or overhanging structures.

3. <u>HARDWARE</u>. Screws, nuts, bolts, hasps, clamps, bars, wire mesh, hinges, and hinge pins must be fastened securely to preclude removal and to ensure visual evidence of tampering. Hardware accessible from outside the security area must be peened, brazed, or spot-welded to preclude removal or the area must be otherwise secured by use of tamper-resistant hardware (e.g., non-removable hinge pins) or by other means as described in the SSP. NOTE: These requirements do not apply to fencing.

4. <u>FENCING</u>. When used to protect security areas designated as LAs or higher, fencing must meet the following requirements.

    a. <u>Fencing Materials and Specifications</u>.

        (1) Chain link fabric consisting of a minimum of No. 11 American Wire Gauge (AWG) or heavier galvanized steel wire with mesh openings not larger than 2 inches (5.08 centimeters) on a side must be used at security areas. This fencing must be topped by three or more strands of barbed wire single or double outriggers. Double outriggers may be topped with coiled barbed wire (or with a barbed tape coil). The direction of the outrigger is at the discretion of the cognizant security authority.

        (2) Overall fence height, excluding barbed wire or barbed tape coil topping, must be a minimum of 7 feet (2.13 meters).

        (3) Fence lines must be kept clear of vegetation, trash, equipment, and other objects that could impede observation or facilitate bridging.

        (4) Gate hardware that if removed would facilitate unauthorized entry must be installed in a manner to mitigate tampering and/or removal (e.g., by brazing, peening, or welding).

        (5) Posts, bracing, and other structural members must be located on the inside of security fences.

        (6) Wire ties used to fasten fence fabric to poles must be of equal tensile strength to that of the fence fabric.

    b. <u>Permanent Security Fencing</u>. When permanent fencing is used to enclose LAs or higher, fencing must meet the following construction requirements.

        (1) Areas under security fencing subject to water flow, such as bridges, culverts, ditches, and swales, must be blocked with wire or steel bars that provide for the passage of floodwater but also provide a penetration delay equal to that of the security fence.

        (2) Depressions where water flow is not a problem must be covered by additional fencing suspended from the lower rail of the main fencing.

        (3)   Fencing must extend to within 2 inches (5.08 centimeters) of firm ground or below the surface if the soil is unstable or subject to erosion.

            (a)   Surfaces must be stabilized in areas where loose sand, shifting soils, or surface waters may cause erosion and thereby assist an intruder in penetrating the area.

            (b)   Where surface stabilization is impossible or impractical, concrete curbs, sills, or a similar type of anchoring device extending below ground level must be provided.

        (4)   Alternate barriers may be used instead of fencing if the penetration resistance of the barrier is equal to or greater than security fencing specified in this chapter.

    c.   <u>Temporary Security Fencing</u>. Temporary barriers may be of any height and material that effectively impedes access to the area. During construction or temporary activities, security fencing must be installed to:

        (1)   exclude unauthorized vehicular and pedestrian traffic from the security area site,

        (2)   restrict authorized vehicular traffic to designated access roads, and

        (3)   comply with site-specific protection goals and operational requirements.

5.   <u>PERIMETER BARRIER GATES</u>. Controls for motorized gates used for entry control points must be located within protective force posts or other locations as described in the SSP. Motorized gates must be designed to facilitate manual operation during power outages.

6.   <u>EXTERIOR WALLS</u>. Walls that constitute exterior barriers of security areas must extend from the floor to the structural ceiling unless equivalent means are used to provide evidence of penetration of the security area or access to the security interest being protected.

7.   <u>CEILING AND FLOORS</u>. Ceilings and floors must be constructed of building materials that offer penetration resistance to, and evidence of, unauthorized entry into the area.

8.   <u>DOORS</u>. Doors, door frames, and door jambs associated with walls serving as barriers must provide the necessary barrier delay required by the SSP. Requirements include the following.

    a.   <u>Penetration Resistance Doors</u>. Doors with transparent glazing material must offer penetration resistance to, and evidence of, unauthorized entry into the area. Doors that serve exclusively as emergency and evacuation exits from security areas must:

      (1)   not be accessible from outside the security area; and

      (2)   comply with NFPA 101.

    b.   <u>Astragals or Mullions</u>. An astragal or mullion must be used where doors used in pairs meet. Door louvers, baffles, or astragals/mullions must be reinforced and immovable from outside the area being protected.

    c.   <u>Visual Access</u>. A sight baffle must be used if visual access is a factor.

9.   <u>WINDOWS</u>. The following design requirements must be applied to security windows when used as physical barriers.

    a.   Windows must offer penetration resistance to, and evidence of, unauthorized entry into the area.

    b.   Frames must be securely anchored in the walls and windows locked from the inside or installed in fixed (non-operable) frames so the panes are not removable from outside the area under protection.

    c.   Visual barriers must be used if visual access is a factor.

10.   <u>MISCELLANEOUS OPENINGS</u>. The following requirements apply to security areas other than GAAs and PPAs. The application to GAAs and PPAs is at the discretion of the cognizant security authority based on a risk assessment.

    a.   <u>Utility and Other Barrier Penetrations and Openings</u>. Physical protection features must be implemented at all locations where miscellaneous openings occur, such as where storm sewers, drainage swales, and site utilities intersect the security boundary or area. Miscellaneous openings/penetrations must be sealed/filled or constricted barriers applied to deter and/or prevent a determined threat. In those instances where a potential audio/video surveillance threat could occur within conference rooms and other similar facilities approved for classified discussions the provisions of DOE M 470.4-4A should be implemented.<u>Criteria</u>. Barriers or alarms are required for all miscellaneous openings for which:

      (1)   the opening is larger than 96 square inches (619.20 square centimeters) in area and larger than 6 inches (15.24 centimeters) in the smallest dimension and/or the opening is located within 18 feet (5.48 meters) of the ground, roof, or ledge of a lower security area;

      (2)   the opening is located within 14 feet (4.26 meters) diagonally or directly opposite a window, fire escape, roof, or other opening in an uncontrolled adjacent building;

(3)   the opening is not visible from another controlled opening in the same barrier; or

(4)   the opening is below a perimeter barrier, which is part of a utility tunnel, pipe chase, exhaust ducts or air handling filter banks penetrating the building, facility, or site.

CHAPTER VII. COMMUNICATIONS, ELECTRICAL POWER AND LIGHTING

1. <u>COMMUNICATIONS</u>. Communications equipment must be provided to facilitate reliable information exchanges between protective force personnel. Security system transmission lines and data must be protected in a graded manner from tampering and substitution.

    a. <u>Loss of Primary Power</u>. Systems must remain operable during the loss and recovery of primary electrical power.

    b. <u>Communication Systems</u>. Protection system communications must support two vital functions: alarm communication/display and protective force (PF) communications. PF communications include the procedures and hardware that enable officers to communicate with each other.

2. <u>ELECTRICAL POWER</u>. Power supply elements located or operating within the confines of the site should be protected from malicious physical attacks based on a documented local site determination of impact. The site must determine the need for auxiliary power based on other safeguards and security interests being protected and document it in the SSP.

3. <u>LIGHTING</u>. Lighting systems must allow for detection and assessment of unauthorized persons. Protective system lighting must:

    a. enable assessment of unauthorized activities and/or persons at pedestrian and vehicular entrances and allow examination of DOE security badges and inspections of personnel, hand-carried items, packages, and vehicles;

    b. be positioned so that PF personnel are not spotlighted, blinded, or silhouetted by the lights, and the lighting placement and design should enhance, not minimize, PF night-vision capabilities;

    c. ensure that compensatory measures identified in the SSP are implemented when the lighting system fails;

    d. be maintained and tested in accordance with locally approved procedures;

    e. not illuminate patrol paths or PF personnel manning fixed posts other than at entry control points;

    f. illuminate the area outside the fence line or barrier so that it will expose anyone approaching the coverage area and limit the vision of anyone outside of the fence or barrier;

    g. complement the electro-optical/closed-circuit television (CCTV) assessment systems;

h.   illuminate the area within the fence/barrier boundary or the exterior of a building;

i.   be configured so that an intruder cannot defeat the system by easily gaining access to the lighting controls and turning-off the system; and

j.   allow for the rapid and reliable assessment of alarms from either the CCTV system or PF personnel.

CHAPTER VIII. SECURE STORAGE

1. <u>GENERAL REQUIREMENTS.</u>

    a. <u>Secure Storage.</u> The storage requirements for classified matter can be found in Information Security policy (see DOE M 470.4-4A).

    b. <u>Access Controls.</u> Access to vaults and vault- type rooms (VTRs) must be strictly controlled and based on an appropriate security clearance and need-to-know.

        (1) Persons without need-to-know and the appropriate security clearance must be escorted at all times.

        (2) Protective measures to mask classified matter must be used before visitors or cleared persons without need-to-know receive access.

        (3) Means of controlling access must be documented in an SSP.

        (4) Access controls at vaults and VTRs must provide logging or recording of all personnel entries and exits including visitors. Logged or recorded entries must include the identification/name and date/time of entry and exit of the individual and the escort as required.

            (a) In vaults and VTRs where entering personnel are restricted from access (e.g., a foyer) to SNM or classified matter, logging entry and exit is not required.

            (b) The cognizant security authority may waive the requirement for repeated logging for personnel whose offices are located within the boundary of the vaults and VTRs. Initial daily entry and final daily exit logging are required.

    c. <u>Miscellaneous Openings.</u> Any miscellaneous openings of a size and shape to permit unauthorized entry [larger than 96 square inches (619.2 square centimeters) in area and more than 6 inches (15.24 centimeters) in its smallest dimension] must be equipped with barriers such as wire mesh, 9-gauge expanded metal, or rigid steel bars at least 0.5 inches (1.3 centimeters) in diameter secured in a way to prevent unauthorized removal e.g., welded vertically and horizontally 6 inches (15.24 centimeters) on center. The rigid steel bars must be securely fastened at both ends to preclude removal. Where used, wire mesh, expanded metal, or rigid steel bars must be mounted so that classified matter or SNM cannot be removed. When pipe or conduit pass through a wall, the annular space between the sleeve and the pipe or conduit must be filled to show evidence of surreptitious removal.

2. <u>VAULTS AND VAULT-TYPE ROOMS.</u> The standards required for construction of vaults and vault-type rooms, other than GSA-approved modular vaults, apply to all new construction, reconstruction, alterations, modifications and repairs.

Vault construction standards must comply with Federal Standard 832, Construction Methods and Materials for Vaults.

Vault-type room construction standards must comply with the requirements of this Manual. The cognizant security authority must approve all construction types and the methods used before the storage of classified matter or S&S interests is authorized.

a. <u>Vaults</u>. A vault must be a penetration-resistant, windowless enclosure that has doors, walls, floor, and roof/ceiling designed and constructed to significantly delay penetration from forced entry and equipped with intrusion detection system devices on openings allowing access. The material thickness must be determined by the requirement for forcible entry delay times for the safeguards and security interest stored within but must not be less than the delay time provided by a minimum 8-inch (20.32-centimeters)-thick reinforced concrete poured in place, with a minimum 28-day compressive strength of 2,500 pounds per square inch (17,237 kilopascal). Technologies such as activated barriers or passive/active denial systems may be used in lieu of thicker concrete when analysis indicates that delay times exceeding that of 8-inch (20.32-centimeters)-thick reinforced concrete are required. The site's analysis of protection measures used must be documented in its site security plan. For new vault construction, Federal Standard 832, Federal Standard Construction Methods and Materials for Vaults must be used.

 (1) Vault Door. A vault door and frame must meet the GSA's highest level of penetration resistance. The lock on the door must be a minimum of a GSA-approved lock.

 (2) Wall Penetrations. Any miscellaneous openings of a size and shape to permit unauthorized entry [larger than 96 square inches (619.2 square centimeters} in area and more than 6 inches (15.24 centimeters) in its smallest dimension] must be equipped with barriers such as wire mesh, 9-gauge expanded metal or rigid steel bars at least 0.5 inches (1.3 centimeters) in diameter secured in a way to prevent unauthorized removal; e.g., welded vertically and horizontally 6 inches (15.24 centimeters) on center. The rigid steel bars must be securely fastened at both ends to preclude removal. Where used, wire mesh, expanded metal, or rigid steel bars must be mounted so that special nuclear material (SNM) cannot be removed. The annular space between the sleeve and the pipe or conduit must be filled to show evidence of surreptitious removal.

 (3) Modular Vaults. A modular vault approved by the GSA may be used in lieu of a vault for the storage of classified matter. The modular vault must be equipped with a GSA-approved vault door with locks and intrusion detection alarms as specified in paragraph 4b of this chapter.

b. <u>Vault-Type Room</u>. The perimeter walls, floors, and ceiling must be permanently constructed and attached to one another. All construction must be done in a manner that provides visual evidence of unauthorized penetration. The walls, floor, ceiling and door and door frame must be constructed of materials which provide comparable penetration resistance. The following standards are required for all new construction, reconstruction, alterations, modifications, and repairs of existing areas.

(1)   Hardware. Hardware must be fastened in such a way to reveal or preclude surreptitious removal and to ensure visual evidence of tampering. Hardware accessible from outside the area must be peened, pinned, brazed, or spot-welded to preclude removal.

(2)   Floors and Walls. Construction materials must offer resistance to and evidence of unauthorized entry into the VTR. If insert-type panels are used, a method must be devised to prevent their removal without leaving visual evidence of tampering.

     (a)   Should any of the outer walls/floors or ceilings be adjacent to space not controlled by DOE, the walls must be constructed of or reinforced with more substantial building materials such as brick, concrete, corrugated metal, wire mesh, etc.

     (b)   If visual access is a factor, barrier walls must be opaque or translucent.

(3)   Windows. Windows that can be routinely opened and are installed at a height of less than 18 feet (5.48 meters) from any point adjacent to the window that would permit unrestricted access must be provided with protective measures to delay or deter entry or to notify the response force of an attempted entry.

     (a)   If visual access is a security concern, the windows must be closed and locked and must be translucent or opaque.

     (b)   During non-working hours, the windows must be closed and securely fastened to preclude surreptitious entry.

(4)   Doors. Doors must be of wood or metal. Windows, door louvers, baffle plates or service panels, or similar openings must be secured on the inside with 18-gauge expanded metal or wire mesh to preclude unauthorized entry. Wooden doors must be of solid core construction, 1.75 inches (4.445 centimeters) thick, or faced on the exterior side with at least 16-gauge sheet metal.

     (a)   If visual access is a security concern, the opening or window must be baffled or must be covered with translucent or opaque coverings.

    (b)   When doors are used in pairs, an astragal must be installed where the doors meet.

    (c)   When door louvers or baffle plates are used, they must be reinforced with 18-gauge expanded metal or wire mesh fastened inside the VTR.

    (5)   Ceilings.

    (a)   When barrier walls do not extend to the true ceiling and a false ceiling is created, the false ceiling must be reinforced with 18-gauge expanded metal or wire mesh to serve as a true ceiling or ceiling tile clips must be secured. When barrier walls do extend to the true ceiling, reinforcements are not required.

    <u>1</u>   Any wire mesh or expanded metal used must overlap the adjoining walls and be secured to show evidence of any tampering.

    <u>2</u>   When ceiling tile clips are used, a minimum of four clips per tile must be installed. If the ceiling tile cannot accommodate four clips, the maximum number of clips that can be accommodated on the tile must be used. The clips must be installed from the interior of the area, and each clip must be mounted to preclude surreptitious entry.

    (b)   In some instances, it may not be practical to erect a solid suspended ceiling as part of the VTR. For example, in VTRs where overhead cranes are used to move bulky equipment, the air-conditioning system may be impeded by the construction of a solid suspended ceiling, or the height of the security interest may make a suspended ceiling impractical. In such cases, special provisions such as motion detection systems must be used to ensure that the area cannot be entered surreptitiously by going over the top of the walls.

3.   <u>VAULT-TYPE ROOM COMPLEX</u>. Vault-type room S&S criteria may be extended to multiple rooms including an entire building. VTR complexes must meet the standards and construction requirements identified in paragraph 2b above.

    a.   Interior walls may extend to a false ceiling and/or raised floor. Interior doors, windows, and openings may exist between different work areas. The requirement to detect unauthorized access may be accomplished through direct visual observation by an individual authorized in the area or through intrusion detection sensors.

DOE M 470.4-2A
7-23-09

VIII-5

b. Protective measures must ensure that the security interest is surrounded by an IDS or that the entire surrounding perimeter (walls, ceiling and floor) is able to detect penetration. For a building within a PA, a perimeter intrusion detection and assessment system that surrounds the entire building perimeter meets the IDS requirement. This does not mitigate the requirement for an IDS within each VTR.

4. <u>INTRUSION DETECTION SYSTEMS</u>. IDSs are required for vaults and VTRs and in some instances where certain types of containers are used to store S&S interests. At vaults and VTRs containing Top Secret, SNM, or open storage of classified information, the IDS must be placed in secure mode when the vault or VTR is unoccupied. In all cases, the IDS must be placed in secure mode at the end of daily operations.

a. <u>Vaults.</u> Doors or openings allowing access into vaults must be equipped with IDS devices. A balanced magnetic switch (BMS) or other equally effective device must be used on each door or movable opening to allow detection of attempted or actual unauthorized access.

b. <u>Vault-Type Rooms</u>. In addition to the requirements listed below, a BMS or equivalent device must be used on each door or movable opening to allow detection of attempted or actual unauthorized access. At a VTR designated for the open storage of classified matter, protective measures must ensure that that the security interest is surrounded by an IDS or that the entire surrounding perimeter (walls, ceiling and floor) is able to detect penetration.

(1) IDS sensors are to be used to detect movement within the VTR envelope, sensor coverage must ensure that the security interest is surrounded by an IDS such that physical access is detected via any credible pathway. Where visual access is a concern, detection must occur prior to the point where visual access becomes possible.

(a) The cognizant security authority may require the installation of sensors in the false floor area (or ceiling) if the distance exceeds 6 inches (15.24 centimeters). If the requirements of this paragraph are not implemented, paragraph (b) must also be considered.

(b) The interests under protection must be considered when not requiring the installation of sensors between the true floor (or ceiling) and the false floor (or ceiling).

(2) Where IDS sensors are used to detect movement within a vault-type room, sensors must provide coverage of credible pathways from the exterior barrier to the matter being protected.

5. <u>SECURITY CONTAINERS</u>. The GSA establishes the national standards and specifications for commercially manufactured security containers or cabinets. Containers purchased after July 14, 1994, must conform to the latest GSA standards and specifications. Steel filing cabinets with rigid metal lock bar and approved three position,

dial-type, changeable combination locks, purchased and approved for storage of SECRET material may continue to be used until October 1, 2012. If steel filing cabinets are used to store classified matter, the supplemental controls specified in DOE M 470.4-4A must be implemented.

    a.   <u>Requirements</u>.

        (1)   Label and Mark. A security container must bear a test certification label on the inside of the locking drawer or door and must be marked "GSA-Approved Security Container" on the outside of the top drawer or door.

        (2)   Maintenance. A history for each security container describing damage sustained and repairs accomplished must be recorded on Optional Form 89, *Maintenance Record for Security Containers/Vault Doors* and retained for the life of the security container.

    b.   <u>Damage and Repair of GSA-Approved Security Containers</u>. Neutralizing lock-outs or repairing any damage that affects the integrity of a security container approved for the storage of classified information must be conducted by cleared or escorted safe technicians or locksmiths.

        (1)   Requirements in Federal Standard 809, *Neutralization and Repair of GSA Approved Containers*, must be met for neutralization and repair of GSA-approved containers and vault doors.

        (2)   Physically modified containers are not approved by GSA.

6.   <u>NON-CONFORMING STORAGE</u>. Non-Conforming Storage is a means of providing equivalent storage protection for classified matter that cannot be protected by established standards and requirements due to size, nature, operational necessity, or other factors. Authority and protection requirements for non-conforming storage are provided in DOE M 470.4-4A.

CHAPTER IX. INTRUSION DETECTION AND ASSESSMENT SYSTEMS

1. <u>GENERAL REQUIREMENTS</u>. The intrusion detection and assessment system is configured to support interior and exterior applications. Intrusion detection and assessment systems and/or visual observation by protective force personnel must be used to protect classified matter, Government property, and SNM to ensure breaches of security barriers or boundaries are detected and alarms annunciate. The systems must be configured so that only authorized personnel may make adjustments.

    a. Intrusion detection and assessment systems must function effectively in all environmental conditions and under all types of lighting conditions or compensatory measures must be implemented.

    b. An effective method must be established for assessing all IDS alarms (e.g., line supervision, intrusion, false, nuisance, system failure, tamper, and radio frequency alarms when radio frequency is used) to determine the cause.

    c. IDS alarms used for the protection of S&S interests must be assessed immediately by either the PF, central alarm station (CAS)/ secondary alarm station (SAS) personnel via closed-circuit television (CCTV), or by other authorized personnel as identified in the SSP.

    d. Response capability to IDS alarms must be provided to protect S&S interests.

    e. The response capability must be provided by assigned PF personnel, by local law enforcement agency, or other authorized personnel as documented in the SSP.

    f. Systems, system components, and critical system elements must be performance-tested at a documented frequency commensurate with the established requirements (see DOE M 470.4-1).

    g. The testing program for systems and system components must be developed and implemented in locally developed security planning documents.

    h. Performance testing must be conducted to validate system effectiveness.

    i. Performance testing should be conducted to determine the proper settings for high detection rates with the lowest possible nuisance alarm rates. Tests should be performed along credible pathways with a low-profile target (crawling) and a higher velocity and profile targets (walking, running, fast-crawl, rolling) or as appropriate given space considerations for interior applications. If assessment is by CCTV, the tests should be conducted under the lowest lighting conditions that are routinely available. The testing should be conducted against the worst case "light to dark ratio" to determine if shadows or dark spots in the field of view degrade assessment viability.

    j. Testing must ensure that the alarm communication line or data link is capable of transmitting an alarm signal and that it has not been compromised.

k. The IDS must be designed, installed, operated, and maintained to ensure that the number of false and nuisance alarms do not reduce system effectiveness.

(1) The false and nuisance threshold rates are determined after analysis and evaluation. The cognizant security authority develops written False Alarm Rates (FAR)/Nuisance Alarm Rates (NAR) parameters based on the analysis and site specific conditions, seeking to achieve "As Low As Reasonably Achievable" (ALARA) levels. However, at a minimum:

(a) Each interior intrusion detection sensor should not have a false or nuisance alarm rate of more than one alarm per 2400 hours of operation while maintaining proper detection sensitivity.

(b) Each exterior intrusion detection sensor should not have a false or nuisance alarm rate of more than one alarm per 24 hours of operation while maintaining proper detection sensitivity.

(c) Interior IDS used to protect munitions/explosives storage igloos/bunkers should not have false or nuisance alarm rates exceeding one alarm per 400 hours of operation while maintaining proper detection sensitivity.

(2) If the alarms can be assessed at all times, either visually or by CCTV, a higher nuisance alarm rate may be tolerated if such alarms do not degrade system effectiveness. Although higher rates may be tolerated, each alarm occurrence, regardless of the cause, must be documented for analysis and trending purposes.

2. INTERIOR IDS REQUIREMENTS. The following requirements apply to interior IDS:

a. Interior Systems. Interior systems must be designed, installed, and maintained to deter adversaries from circumventing the detection system.

(1) Interior systems must be installed to eliminate gaps in detection coverage.

(2) The IDS must be tested when installed and annually (at least every 12 months) thereafter.

(3) If testing indicates degradation of the IDS, it must be repaired and retested.

(4) Interior IDSs may be used as compensatory measures for unattended entry/exit points, utility ducts, or other openings meeting the unattended openings requirements contained in this Manual.

b. Balanced Magnetic Switches. BMSs must initiate an alarm upon attempted substitution of an external magnetic field when the switch is in the normal secured position and whenever the leading edge of the door is moved 1 inch (2.5 centimeters) from the door jamb.

c.   Volumetric Devices. Tests for volumetric interior IDSs must consider a range of tests; i.e., walk tests, voltage variation, temperature and humidity, electromagnetic susceptibility, vibration, standby power, handling shock tests.

d.   Functional Testing. A functional test, in conformance with the manufacturer's specification, should be performed prior to acceptance of the installed system and thereafter as determined necessary by the facility.

e.   Performance Testing. Interior IDS must be performance tested in accordance with locally established procedures, (i.e., walking, running, jumping, crawling, or rolling along the path to the item being protected) at a documented frequency.

3.   EXTERIOR IDS REQUIREMENTS.

a.   Exterior IDS. Exterior IDSs must be designed, where economically feasible, with independent redundant data communication paths for protecting DOE S&S interests. The paths must be documented in an SSP or protection procedures, consistent with Table 1, Line Supervision Protection.

b.   Detection Capability. The IDS must be capable of detecting an individual crossing the detection zone by walking, crawling, jumping, running, or rolling, or climbing the fence at any point in the detection zone, with a detection probability of 90 percent and confidence level of 95 percent.

      (1)   The IDS must be tested when installed and annually (at least every 12 months) thereafter to validate that it meets detection probability and confidence level requirements.

      (2)   Any time the IDS falls below the required probability of detection, the IDS must be repaired and retested.

      (3)   When calculating detection probability for multiple sensor technology systems, detection is assumed if any of the sensors/zones report an intrusion. Multiple sensor technology systems may include taut wire, microwave, infra-red, ported coax, and laser components.

c.   Miscellaneous Openings. For all openings in exterior barriers, unattended gates and/or entry/exit points, culverts and sewers, that meet the unattended opening criteria of Chapter VI, intrusion detection capabilities must be as effective as the rest of the perimeter IDS.

d.   Perimeter Alarm/Detection and Assessment System. Perimeter Alarm/Detection and Assessment systems must be:

        (1)   designed to cover the entire perimeter without a gap in detection, including the sides and tops of structures situated within;

        (2)   located such that the length of each detection zone is consistent with the characteristics of the sensors used in that zone and the topography;

        (3)   designed, installed, and maintained to deter adversaries from circumventing the detection system;

        (4)   provided with an isolation zone at least 20 feet (6 meters) wide and clear of fabricated or natural objects that would interfere with operation of detection systems or the effectiveness of the assessment;

        (5)   free of wires, piping, poles, and similar objects that could be used to assist an intruder traversing the isolation zone or that could assist in the undetected ingress or egress of an adversary or matter; and

        (6)   constructed in a manner that detects and deters the use of wire, piping, poles, etc., that cannot be eliminated from the isolation zone.

    e.   <u>Alarm Zone Degradation</u>. Each alarm zone must be kept free of snow, ice, grass, weeds, debris, wildlife, and any other item that may degrade the effectiveness of the system. When this cannot be accomplished and detection capabilities become degraded, compensatory measures are required.

4.   <u>RADIO FREQUENCY ALARM COMMUNICATIONS</u>. Radio frequency alarm communications are appropriate when used for the protection of government property and classified matter. RF communications may also be used in the protection of S&S interests in emergency and temporary situations. In addition RF may be used as part of a site's early warning system. The use of RF communications in the protection of SNM in other than a temporary or emergency situation are described in the appendices of this manual. An IDS may use radio frequency communications to transmit alarm and other data for alarms, video, and other data utilized by the IDS provided:

    a.   The data being transmitted are not classified.

    b.   The data being transmitted are protected consistent with the program office cyber security plan and DOE requirements (see Chapter 9, DOE M 200.1-1, *Telecommunications Security Manual*, dated 2-15-00).

5.   <u>PROTECTION OF IDSs</u>.

    a.   <u>General Requirements</u>.

        (1)   IDS equipment should be protected in a graded manner consistent with the security interest being protected.

(2) System components protecting Top Secret, vital equipment, SCIF and SAPF activities must be protected with tamper indication in both the access and the secure modes. Tamper indication is required for intrusion detection/alarm devices. Tamper switch wiring must be as listed below.

(a) Communication links, DGP/field processors and associated equipment must be provided with tamper detection switches on enclosure covers wired to a 24-hour circuit. The wiring must be protected from unauthorized access per UL Standard 681.

(b) All tamper switches (e.g., senors, processors, cable terminal boxes, control units, etc.) must be wired into a 24-hour circuit. More than one switch may be wired to a single circuit if the switches are located in the same general area.

(c) The switches may be wired as part of the line supervision circuit per UL Standard 681. However, tamper switches may be wired independent of line supervision circuits for hazardous areas, radiological controlled areas, SNM storage vaults, and other areas where testing and maintenance cost would be offset by using a separate circuit.

(3) Commercial Central Alarm Station Service firms must issue a current Underwriter's Laboratory (UL) certification commensurate with the contracted service and must maintain this UL certification as long as the service is provided to the facility. For the protection of classified matter UL 2050, National Industrial Security Service standard, should be implemented and a certificate issued for compliance with the UL standard. For other non-classified matter applications, Proprietary Burglar-Alarm Units and Systems- UL 1076, should be implemented and a certificate issued for compliance with the UL standard.

b. Enclosures and Junction Boxes. Permanent junction boxes, field distribution boxes, cable terminal boxes, and cabinets (equipment that terminates, splices, and groups interior or exterior IDS input or that could allow tampering, spoofing, bypassing, or other system sabotage) must be afforded tamper protection. When a box is secured by a Level IV locking device, the keys may be master keyed. Tamper switches must provide a tamper indication to the annunciators. Manholes and other enclosures, if serving as a junction box for data communication cables, must be protected from unauthorized access.

c. Line Supervision. Line supervision is required for IDSs protecting S&S interests. For property protection areas, line supervision may be provided consistent with a documented cost/benefit analysis as determined by the cognizant security authority. Where data encryption is used, key changes must be made annually (at least every 12 months) and whenever compromise is suspected. The requirements for line supervision are listed in Table 1, Line Supervision Protection. In the event line security is not available the equipment that is utilized to transmit and receive signals between the protected area and the monitoring location should comply with either UL 1076 or UL 1610.

(1)   Line Supervision Options. Different combinations of line supervision are allowed depending on link routing:

    (a)   An alarm communication link remaining within the security area and alarm communication link going through a lower security area.

    (b)   Line supervision is required for the two primary segments of alarm data transmission: from sensor to data gathering panel (DGP)/field processor and from DGP/field processor to DGP/field processor or the central processing unit.

(2)   Classes of Line Supervision. Performance-based definitions are listed below in descending order of protection.

    (a)   In general, alarm data encryption, pseudo-random polling or unencrypted data transmission are the preferred UL Classes (Class A through C), apply to alarm communication links between DGPs/field processors, between DGPs/field processors and central alarm computers or alarm annunciator panels, and between computers.

        <u>1</u>   For Class A, the data transmission must comply with DOE requirements (see Chapter 9, DOE M 200.1-1, *Telecommunications Security Manual*, dated 2-15-00).

        <u>2</u>   For Class B, data must be transmitted by one of the following:

            <u>a</u>   encryption using a proprietary encryption scheme that results in non-repetitive communications,

            <u>b</u>   pseudo-random polling scheme, non-encryption over fiber optic cable enclosed in conduit, or

            <u>c</u>   non-encryption over fiber optic cable monitored by an optical supervision system.

        <u>3</u>   For Class C, unencrypted data transmissions include:

            <u>a</u>   RS-232, RS-485, etc., data transmission standard,

            <u>b</u>   standard repetitive polling schemes, and

<u>c</u> exception reporting with repetitive polling for health checks.

(b) Classes D through F apply to data transmission through changes in the analog signal. In general, Classes D through F apply to alarm communication links between a sensor and a field processor.

<u>1</u> Class D supervision must combine various frequencies of alternating current (AC), be pulsed direct current (DC) or be a combination of AC and DC.

<u>2</u> Class E supervision must be an AC signal.

<u>3</u> Class F supervision must be a DC signal.

(3) Protecting Alarm Wiring. Physical protection of alarm wiring must be as listed below.

(a) Protection for communication links must meet the supervised circuit requirements for the National Electric Code for protection from damage (see UL Standard 681).

(b) Protection for wiring between the sensor and the field processor using Class F line supervision must be protected from access. For alarm wiring protecting Top Secret, and vital equipment, protection for wiring between the sensor and the DGP/field processor using Class F line supervision must be protected from access when the DGP/field processor is outside the area being protected. Acceptable methods for protecting alarm system wiring are as follows:

<u>1</u> a totally concealed or embedded conduit system;

<u>2</u> junction boxes, pull boxes and other openings sealed by welding, epoxy-sealed threads, locked cover plates, tamper-resistant screws, or tamper alarm switches;

<u>3</u> alarm coverage of all wiring, or;

<u>4</u> armored cable/wire or threaded conduit.

d. <u>Alarm Annunciation and Response</u>.

(1) Line supervision alarms Classes A through C must annunciate in both the CAS and the SAS indicating the type of alarm (data error, loss of communication, tamper, etc.) and the affected equipment.

(2) Sensor to DGP/field processor (Classes C through F) line supervision alarms must annunciate in both the CAS and SAS, indicating the sensor or sensors affected.

(3) PF personnel must be put on alert, and system maintenance personnel must be notified, when line supervision alarms indicate a loss of a communications path of a redundant system.

(4) Line supervision alarm, tamper alarm, or radio frequency alarm events (e.g., "statement-of-health" alarm, sensor alarm, tamper alarm, and radio frequency jamming indications) must be treated the same as an intrusion alarm for the area being protected.

(5) Maintenance personnel must be notified of a tamper or line supervision alarm, and the alarm condition must be assessed by PF response personnel.

(a) Compensatory measures must be implemented to protect the alarmed location until required testing and repairs are completed.

(b) Tamper and line supervision alarms must be tested to verify effectiveness. Alarm system components being protected by the tamper alarm, e.g., BMS, microwave, passive infrared, must be tested through physical actuation (see Table 1. Line Supervision Protection).

Table 1. Line Supervision Protection

Communication Lines between a Field Processor and Field Processor or a Central Processor				
	Vital Equipment or Top Secret Classified Matter	Classified Matter Secret and below	Maximum Internal System communications supervision interval	Required Manual Testing
	Class of Supervision	Class of Supervision	(ALL)	(ALL)
Routed within the alarm area	C	C	15 minutes	Annually*
Routed through a lower security area	B	C	10 minutes	Annually*
Routed through an unsecured area	A	B	5 minutes	Annually*
Wiring from the Sensor to the Data Gathering Panel (DGP)				
All field wiring	F	F	Continuously	Annually*

*At least every 12 months

6.   <u>ELECTRICAL POWER</u>. Electrical power to supply the intrusion detection and assessment systems should be provided to assure continuous system availability and operation. The scope of the primary and auxiliary power sources are as follows.

    a.   <u>Primary Power</u>. All IDS must have primary power from normal onsite power. The power source must contain a switching capability for component and total system testing. This testing can be used to determine the capacity and source of the required auxiliary power. The following system elements should be considered in configuring the power requirements.

        (1)   Alarm data networks and communication systems should receive primary power directly from the onsite power distribution system. When the facility does not receive its power from an internal distribution system, power would come directly from the public utility.

        (2)   Alarm control panels, alarm management systems and automated information systems or associated critical components must be connected to an uninterruptible power supply or auxiliary power.

    b.   <u>Auxiliary-Uninterruptible Power</u>. Auxiliary or uninterruptible power sources should be provided for alarm systems requiring continuous power and for systems that, if interrupted, would degrade or compromise the protection afforded the asset.

7.   <u>ASSESSMENT OF IDS ALARMS</u>. An effective method must be established for assessing IDS alarms (e.g., line supervision, intrusion, false, nuisance, system failures, tamper, and radio frequency when radio frequency is used).

    a.   Alarms must be assessed immediately by either the PF or by a central alarm monitoring station personnel using CCTV.

    b.   CCTV assessment cameras used as primary assessment for alarms should be fixed (i.e., not pan or tilt) with fixed focal length lenses or may have a zoom capability.

CHAPTER X. ENTRY/EXIT SCREENING

1.   GENERAL. With the exception of Protected and Material Access Areas where inspection is mandatory, random inspections are to be conducted at other designated security area boundaries. The cognizant security authority must determine the locations and scope of the screening program at other than PA and MA boundaries. An inspection program must be configured to detect prohibited and controlled articles before being brought into DOE facilities. These programs are to protect Department assets and interests from unauthorized removal without management authorization. Any entry/exit inspection program must be documented in an SSP or procedure.

      a.   Passage of individuals, vehicles, and/or packages or mail through entry control point inspection equipment must be observed and controlled by trained designated personnel.

      b.   Inspection equipment can include handheld and/or portable detectors, metal detectors, special nuclear material detectors, explosive detectors, and x-ray systems and must assist security personnel in ensuring that prohibited and controlled articles will be detected before being brought into or removed from DOE facilities.

      c.   Entrance inspections of personnel, vehicles, packages, and hand-carried items must be performed to deter and detect prohibited and controlled articles. Formally established inspection rates are to be issued by the cognizant security authority.

          (1)   Bypass routes around inspection equipment must be closed or monitored to deter unauthorized passage of personnel and hand-carried articles.

          (2)   Uninterrupted power must be provided to all inspection equipment. In those instances where uninterrupted power is not practical, there must be locally developed procedures to provide alternative measures for conducting entry/exit screening when loss of electrical power occurs.

          (3)   Measures are to be instituted to correctly maintain control settings on all entry/exit control point inspection equipment.

          (4)   Equipment, to include portal monitors, must have audible and visual alarms monitored by on-post trained personnel.

          (5)   Ingress/egress points must be designed to preclude commingling of searched and unsearched personnel.

2.   ENTRY/EXIT INSPECTIONS.

      a.   Explosives Detection.

          (1)   Sites must analyze their facilities to determine the potential for an adversary to use explosives to affect consequences such as sabotage or

theft of DOE assets or fatalities and show that sufficient protective measures have been implemented to result in a low risk of a successful attack. Protective measures may include the integration of various technologies, screening of people, packages, and vehicles as well as the hardening of facilities and other assets to be able to withstand an attack from explosives. This analysis must be included in the overall protection planning process (see DOE M 470.4-1).

(2)   If the analysis determines that explosive detection is required, explosive detection equipment must ensure that explosives are not introduced without appropriate authorization. The SSP or procedure must document the analysis that establishes a facility's capability to detect explosives and provide protection against the malicious use of explosives.

(3)   Documentation must include the rationale for explosive detection equipment/systems selection, deployment, and use.

(4)   Security personnel procedures for explosive detection equipment must be approved by the cognizant security authority.

b.   Metal Detection must be used in the entry process at designated security area boundaries. The cognizant security authority must designate the security area location for the conduct of the screening.

(1)   Metal detectors must ensure weapons are not introduced without authorization.

(2)   Metal detectors used for protected area entry inspection must detect test weapons listed in Chapter V.

(3)   The site must implement the performance testing procedures and test objects or the standards cited in Chapter V.

c.   X-ray Machines may be used to supplement metal detectors and protective personnel hand searches for prohibited and controlled articles. X-ray machines must provide a discernable image of the prohibited and controlled article (see Chapter V).

d.   SNM Detectors used in the inspection process must ensure SNM is not removed without authorization. SNM detectors used in the inspection process must be tested using trace elements that depict the type of material located within the security area. The thresholds must be consistent with the SNM type, form, quantity, attractiveness level, size, configuration, portability, and credible diversion amounts of the articles or property contained within the area.

e.   Personnel, Vehicles, and Hand-Carried Items including packages, briefcases, purses, and lunch containers are to be inspected to deter and detect unauthorized removal of classified matter or other safeguards and security interests from designated security areas.

(1)   Explosive vapor detectors and metal detectors should be used in a combination that precludes the opportunity to defeat the detectors individually at designated area boundaries and when used to inspect personnel for explosives or other prohibited/controlled articles.

(2)   Metal detectors used in the exit inspection process must ensure shielded material is not removed without authorization.

(3)   Specific inspection procedures and response to alarms with limitations and thresholds for the various detectors must be established and documented in the SSP or procedure.

(4)   Exit inspection procedures must be written to ensure:

    (a)   The identification of detection thresholds for the various specified threats and shielding. The thresholds must be consistent with the type, form, quantity, attractiveness level, size, configuration, portability, and credible diversion amounts of material contained within the area.

    (b)   The conduct of random exit inspections at a facility boundary, when a site perimeter boundary encompasses a sensitive area. The frequency must be determined by DOE line management.

f.   Entry Control Point Systems must allow the authorized entry and exit of personnel while detecting prohibited and controlled articles. Entry control point configuration must have separate material package inspection areas/stations for inspecting personnel, packages, and hand-carried items. The following design criteria apply:

(1)   Entry/exit point inspection monitors must be collocated with designated security posts to facilitate the initiation of a response to an alarm.

(2)   Security posts must be designed with an unobstructed view to facilitate observation of any attempt to bypass systems.

(3)   Security structures should consider the requirements in Appendix B.

(4)   Entrances/exits must be alarmed with intrusion detection sensors or controlled at all times to notify of unauthorized use.

APPENDIX A. PROTECTION OF CATEGORY III AND IV SPECIAL NUCLEAR MATERIAL

This Appendix contains the physical protection requirements for Category III and IV quantities of special nuclear material. These requirements are in addition to those physical protection requirements outlined in the base Manual.

CHAPTER A-I. PROTECTION OF
CATEGORY III AND IV SPECIAL NUCLEAR MATERIAL

1. <u>GENERAL REQUIREMENTS</u>. This Appendix contains the requirements for protecting Category III and IV quantities of special nuclear material (SNM). The priority of protection measures must be designed to prevent malevolent acts such as theft, diversion, and radiological sabotage and to respond to adverse conditions such as emergencies caused by acts of nature.

    a. A facility must not possess, receive, process, transport, or store SNM until that facility has been cleared (see DOE M 470.4-1, *Safeguards and Security Program Planning and Management*, dated 8-26-05).

    b. Physical protection for each category of SNM must consider the following factors: quantities, chemical forms, and isotopic composition purities; ease of separation, accessibility, concealment, portability; radioactivity; and self-protecting features (see DOE M 470.4-6 Chg 1, and 10 CFR Part 73, Physical Protection of Plants and Materials, relative to self-protecting).

    c. The protection of nuclear material production, reactors, and fuel must be commensurate with the category of SNM.

    d. SNM, parts, or explosives that are classified must receive the physical protection required by the higher level of classification or category of SNM, whichever is the more stringent.

2. <u>CATEGORY III QUANTITIES OF SNM</u>. The following requirements apply.

    a. <u>In Use or Processing</u>. Category III quantities of SNM must be used or processed in an access controlled security area within at least a limited area (LA) and in accordance with local security procedures approved by the DOE cognizant security authority.

    b. <u>Storage</u>. Category III quantities of SNM must be stored within a locked security container or room, either of which must be located within at least an LA. The container or room must be under the protection of an intrusion detection system or protective force patrol physical check at least every 8 hours.

3. <u>CATEGORY IV QUANTITIES OF SNM</u>. The following requirements apply.

    a. <u>In Use or Processing</u>. Category IV quantities of SNM must be used or processed within at least a property protection area and in accordance with local security procedures approved by the DOE cognizant security authority.

    b. <u>Storage</u>. Category IV quantities of SNM must be stored in a locked area within at least a property protection area, and procedures must be documented in an approved SSP.

4.   <u>LIMITED AREAS</u>. LAs are security areas that are established to protect classified matter and Category III quantities of SNM and to serve as a concentric layer of protection. In addition to the requirements for a PPA, the following apply to an LA.

    a.   <u>General Requirements</u>. LAs are defined by physical barriers encompassing the designated space and access controls to ensure that only authorized personnel are allowed to enter the area.

    b.   <u>Access Control</u>. Access controls must be in place to ensure that only appropriately cleared and authorized personnel are permitted unescorted access to the LA. Access must be based on an individual's need-to-know to perform official duties, validation of the individual's security clearance, and the presentation of a DOE security badge. Access must be controlled when going from one security area into another security area with increased protection requirements. Where practical, automated access control systems must be used in place of PF or other authorized personnel to control access into security areas.

        (1)   If automated access control equipment is used, a DOE security badge must be used to access electronically stored information relevant to the badge and badge holder.

        (2)   Entry control points for vehicle and pedestrian access to security areas must provide the same level of protection as that provided at all other points along the security perimeter.

        (3)   Entry control points must be structurally hardened to meet site-specific criteria as documented in the SSP.

        (4)   Exits from security areas must satisfy life safety requirements of National Fire Protection Association (NFPA) 101, *Safety to Life from Fire in Buildings and Structures*. Some exits may be provided for emergency use only.

        (5)   Security area entrances and exits must be equipped with doors, gates, rails, or other movable barriers that direct and control the movement of personnel or vehicles through designated control points.

        (6)   Door locks and latches used on security area perimeters must meet life safety requirements of NFPA 101.

        (7)   Automated gates must be designed to allow manual operation during power outages or mechanism failures. Where automated gates are used to control vehicular access to a security area, the gates and openings must be constructed to permit operation from a monitoring/control point or from other manned security posts.

(8)   Site specific requirements and procedures for visitor logs must be approved by the cognizant security authority. If visitor logs are to be used at the PPA, the requirements set forth in Chapter II are to be followed.

c.   <u>Personnel Access</u>.

(1)   Escort Ratios. The cognizant security authority must establish escort-to-visitor ratios in a graded manner for each security area.

(2)   Escort Responsibilities. Any person permitted to enter a security area who does not possess a security clearance at the appropriate level must be escorted at all times by an appropriately cleared and knowledgeable individual trained in local escort procedures.

    (a)   Escorts must ensure measures are taken to prevent compromise of S&S interests.

    (b)   The escort must ensure the visitor has a need-to-know for the security area or the S&S interests.

(3)   Access Validation. Validation must occur at LA entry control points.

    (a)   The identity and security clearance held by each person seeking entry must be validated by appropriately authorized personnel, automated systems, or other means documented in the SSP.

    (b)   Where practicable, PF personnel will not be used to control access to LAs.

(4)   "Piggybacking." The following requirements must be documented in the SSP if piggybacking into LAs is permitted.

    (a)   Personnel with the appropriate security clearance may vouch for another person with the required security clearance to "piggyback" into an LA.

    (b)   Authorized personnel permitting the entry of another person must inspect the individual's DOE security badge to ensure that it bears a likeness of the individual and that he or she has identified, by badge marking, the proper security clearance. Authorized individuals entering an LA, when PF personnel are not controlling access, are responsible and must ensure that unauthorized individuals do not enter ("piggyback").

(5)   Automated Access Control Systems. Automated access control systems may be used if the following requirements are met.

(a) Automated access controls used for access to a security area must verify that the security clearance and the DOE security badge are valid (i.e., that the badge data read by the system match the data assigned to the badge holder). Badges may be validated by means of a personal identification number (PIN) or other approved means as stipulated in the SSP.

(b) When remote, unattended, automated access control system entry control points are used for access to security areas, the barrier must be resistant to bypass. The unattended entry control point should have closed-circuit television system coverage.

(c) Automated control system alarms (e.g., annunciation of a door alarm, duress alarm, tamper alarm, or anti-passback indication feature) must be treated as an intrusion alarm for the area being protected.

(d) Personnel or other protective measures are required to protect PINs, card reader access transactions, displays (e.g., badge-encoded data), and keypad devices. The process of inputting, storing, displaying, or recording verification data must ensure the data are protected in accordance with the SSP.

(e) The system must record all attempts at access to include unsuccessful, unauthorized, and authorized.

(f) Door locks opened by badge readers must be designed to relock immediately after the door has closed.

(g) Transmission lines that carry security clearance and personal identification or verification data between devices/equipment must be protected in accordance with the SSP.

(h) Records reflecting active assignments of DOE security badges, PINs, security clearance, and similar system-related records must be maintained. Records of personnel removed from the system must be retained for 1 year, unless a longer period is specified by other requirements. Personal data must be protected (see 5 U.S.C. 552a).

(i) Badge reader boxes, control lines, and junction boxes should have line supervision or tamper indication or be equipped with tamper-resistant devices. Field processors or multiplexers and other similar equipment must be tamper-alarmed or secured by a means that precludes surreptitious tampering with the equipment.

       (j)   Uninterrupted power supply or compensatory measures must be provided at installations where continuous operation is required.

   (6)   Vehicle Access.

       (a)   DOE cognizant security authority approval for non-Government vehicles, which includes privately owned, to access LAs must be documented in the SSP. Additional factors to be considered are navigation systems, vehicle mounted back-up cameras, computers and cell phones.

       (b)   Government-owned or -leased vehicles may be admitted only when on official business and only when operated by properly cleared and authorized drivers or when the drivers are escorted by properly cleared and authorized personnel.

       (c)   The SSP must identify procedures for inspection of, and access by, service and delivery vehicles.

       (d)   All personnel within a vehicle are required to produce DOE security badges when accessing an LA.

       (e)   When a remote automated access control system is used for vehicle access control, it must verify that the operator or the escort has a valid DOE security badge (e.g., the badge data read by the system must match the data assigned to the badge holder) and a valid security clearance.

  d.   Emergency Personnel and Vehicles. Emergency personnel and vehicles may be authorized for immediate entry to the LA in response to an emergency if conditions and procedures for immediate entry are documented in the SSP.

   (1)   If the emergency condition prevents an exit inspection before departing the site, an escort must be provided, and both personnel and emergency vehicles must be inspected as soon as the emergency is over. If an escort is not provided, provisions must be made for continuous surveillance of all emergency vehicles that enter the LA.

   (2)   As described in DOE M 470.4-4A, *Information Security*, local procedures must be developed for safeguarding classified matter from inadvertent access, by uncleared personnel, or cleared persons who do not have a need-to-know, during emergencies.

  e.   Inspection Program. Entry/exit inspections are required to ensure that prohibited and controlled articles are not introduced without authorization. Likewise such programs must ensure S&S interests are not removed from DOE facilities. Application of entry/exit inspections at locations other than PA and MA boundaries is at the discretion of DOE line management. This discretion extends to security areas containing Category III and IV SNM. The inspection process and locations where inspections are to be conducted must be documented in the SSP. Consideration should be given to conducting these inspections before entry to an LA and after exit from an LA. An inspection program must be established by the cognizant security authority and documented in the SSP.

f. Intrusion Detection. A determination should be made as to the application of electronic physical protection systems. The scope and configuration of these systems are described in Chapter IX. Signs. Signs must be posted to convey information on the Atomic Weapons and Special Nuclear Materials Rewards Act (P.L. 84-165, as amended by P.L. 93-377); prohibited and controlled articles; the inspection of vehicles, packages, hand-carried items, and persons entering or exiting the security area; the use of video surveillance equipment; and trespassing (see 42 U.S.C. Section 2278a).

5. EXCLUSION AREAS (EAs). EAs are security areas that are established to protect classified matter where an individual's mere presence may result in access to classified matter. In addition to requirements for an LA, the following apply to an EA.

a. General Requirements. The boundaries of EAs must be encompassed by physical barriers and be located within the minimum of an LA.

b. Access Control. In addition to the requirements for an LA the following requirements apply to access to an EA:

(1) Individuals permitted unescorted access must have the appropriate access authorizations and a need-to-know consistent with the classified matter to which they have access by virtue of their presence in the EA.

(2) Individuals without the appropriate security clearance and need-to-know must be escorted by a knowledgeable individual who must ensure measures are taken to prevent compromise of classified matter.

(3) Visitor logs must be used for EAs, PAs, and MAAs.

c. Intrusion Detection.

(1) Unauthorized entry into the EA must be detected.

(2) When the exclusion area is unoccupied, and classified matter is not secured in a security container, then the EA must at a minimum, meet the requirements of a vault-type room (VTR).

CHAPTER A-II. ALARM MANAGEMENT AND CONTROL SYSTEM

1. <u>GENERAL REQUIREMENTS</u>. This chapter establishes requirements for integrated physical protection systems protecting Category III SNM and if used for Category IV SNM. When intrusion detection system (IDS) sensors are used to protect safeguards and security (S&S) interests the sensors must annunciate directly to alarm stations when an alarm is activated.

2. <u>ALARM STATIONS</u>. Alarm stations must provide a capability for monitoring and assessing alarms and initiating responses to S&S events.

   a. Alarm station personnel must be knowledgeable of the area being protected and the emergency notification procedures. Knowledge of the area does not encompass the operations contained therein or what is stored or processed. As an example, area knowledge would involve the building alarm configuration, room numbers within the structure, pedestrian and vehicle entry points, etc.

   b. Tamper and supervisory alarms must be assessed by authorized personnel and technical/maintenance support personnel in accordance with local procedures.

   c. Alarm stations must indicate the status of the systems and annunciate a status change. The system must indicate the type and location of the alarm.

   d. Records must be kept of each alarm received in the alarm station and of any maintenance activities conducted on the alarm system or any of the related components.

   e. Personnel manning the alarm station must possess an appropriate security clearance (i.e., Q or L) commensurate with the most sensitive interest under the protection of the alarm station.

   f. Access control systems must ensure admission of authorized personnel only.

   g. Alarms must annunciate both audibly and visibly to an alarm station.

   h. Multiple alarms must be prioritized based on the importance of the S&S interests.

3. <u>COMMERCIAL CENTRAL ALARM STATIONS</u>. Commercial alarms service firms must issue a current Underwriter's Laboratory (UL) certification commensurate with the contracted service and must maintain this UL certification as long as the service is provided to the facility. For the protection of classified matter UL 2050, National Industrial Security Service standard, should be implemented and a certificate issued for compliance with the UL standard.

CHAPTER A-III. INTRUSION DETECTION AND ASSESSMENT SYSTEMS

1. PROTECTING SPECIAL NUCLEAR MATERIAL. Intrusion detection and assessment systems and/or visual observations by protective force (PF) personnel must be used to protect SNM and classified matter to ensure breaches of security barriers or boundaries are detected and alarms annunciate. The following requirements apply for alarms protecting Category III, and when used for protecting Category IV quantities of SNM. Intrusion detection and assessment must be conducted in accordance with the site security plan. Appendix C, *Safeguards and Security Alarm Management and Control Systems* describes technical approaches for the employment of intrusion detection and alarm systems.

2. INTERIOR INTRUSION DETECTION SYSTEM. When used to protect either Category of SNM, IDSs must be configured to:

    a. detect unauthorized access to Category III and IV quantities of SNM;

    b. be compatible with other interior and exterior alarm devices and systems;

    c. automatically activate an alarm to notify of a changed security condition;

    d. function effectively in all environmental conditions;

    e. provide alarm communication line supervision;

    f. provide tamper protection on all alarm devices and alarm data gathering panels,

    g. have a false and nuisance alarm rate as described in Chapter IX of this Manual, while maintaining proper detection sensitivity; and

    h. report alarm conditions to a dedicated location that facilitates continuous monitoring by designated, trained PF or security personnel.

3. EXTERIOR IDS. When used for either Category of SNM, exterior IDSs must be configured to:

    a. detect unauthorized access to Category III and IV quantities of SNM;

    b. compliment the interior IDS;

    c. automatically activate an alarm to notify of a changed security condition;

    d. function effectively in all environmental conditions;

    e. provide alarm communication line supervision;

    f. provide tamper protection on all alarm devices and alarm data gathering panels;

g.   have a false and nuisance alarm rate as described in Chapter IX of this Manual, while maintaining proper detection sensitivity;

h.   report alarm conditions to a dedicated location which facilitates continuous monitoring and assessment by designated trained PF or security administrative personnel; and

i.   The cognizant security authority develops the FAR/NAR standards based on site specific systems to achieve a Low As Responsible Achievable (ALARA) levels.

4.   ASSESSMENT SYSTEMS. An alarm assessment system allows security personnel to determine rapidly whether an intrusion has taken place at a remote location. When used, assessment systems must be configured as an element of the total IDS along with the required complimentary lighting.

a.   A basic assessment system is composed of CCTV cameras positioned at strategic points covering the intrusion detection devices/zones, video display monitors located at a central location, and various transmission and switching systems connecting CCTV cameras to monitors and video recording devices.

b.   The lighting must allow for the fast and reliable assessment of alarms from either the CCTV system or PF personnel as defined in the SSP.

5.   PERFORMANCE TESTING. Systems and system elements are to be performance tested at a documented frequency (see DOE M 470.4-1). The testing program must be implemented in locally prepared planning or procedural documents.

6.   MAINTENANCE. Corrective maintenance procedures for supporting security related systems and subsystems protecting Category III and IV quantities of SNM, must be approved by line management and prescribed in the site's operation procedures.

a.   A scope to preparing corrective maintenance procedures can be found in Chapter V of the base manual.

b.   Preventative maintenance must be performed on critical systems, subsystems and components in conformance with manufacturer's specifications and/or local procedures.

c.   Maintenance personnel must be notified of a tamper or line supervisions alarm, and the alarm condition must be assessed by PF response personnel.

      Tamper and line supervision alarms must be tested to verify effectiveness. BMS, microwave, passive infrared, buried line sensors and DGP/alarm processing panels, must be tested through physical activation of the switch (see Table A-1, Line Supervision Protection).

Table A-1. Line Supervision Protection

Communication Lines between a Field Processor and Field Processor or a Central Processor				
	Cat I or II SNM, Class of Supervision	Cat III or IV SNM, Classified Matter Secret and below Class of Supervision	Maximum Internal System communications supervision interval (ALL)	Required Manual Testing (ALL)
Routed within the alarm area	C	C	15 Minutes	Annually*
Routed through a lower security area	B	C	10 minutes	Annually*
Routed through an unsecured area	A	B	5 minutes	Annually*
Wiring from the Sensor to the Data Gathering Panel (DGP)				
All field wiring	F	F	Continuously	Annually*

*At least every 12 months

CHAPTER A-IV. COMMUNICATIONS

1. RADIO FREQUENCY ALARM COMMUNICATIONS FOR INTRUSION DETECTION SYSTEMS. IDS may use radio frequency communications to transmit alarm and other data for alarms, video, early warning devices, and other data utilized by the IDS provided:

    a. The data being transmitted are not classified.

    b. The data being transmitted are protected consistent with the program office cyber security plan and DOE requirements (see Chapter 9, DOE M 200.1-1, *Telecommunications Security Manual*, dated 2-15-00).

2. OTHER REQUIREMENTS. Radio frequency communications for IDS must also meet the following requirements.

    a. Provide self-checking alarm communication paths that annunciate system failure in the alarm stations.

    b. Ensure that the statement-of-health interval allows for an assessment and response.

    c. Provide unique status change messages for alarm, tamper, and power conditions.

    d. Provide an operator-initiated polling feature to allow a check of communication link integrity.

    e. Have tamper-resistant or tamper-switch alarm transmitters.

    f. Have auxiliary power for critical components until power can be restored or compensatory measures can be implemented.

    g. Not produce spurious signals that interfere with other security system components.

    h. Provide a unique electronic address code for each transmitter/receiver pair.

    i. Provide a means of interfacing with the alarm annunciation system (e.g., the alarm station or central alarm station).

    j. Provide reliable communications in all weather conditions.

    k. Ensure system integrity is maintained (i.e., not diminished) during multiple alarms.

    l. Operate on authorized frequency bands.

m.   Not change status on a network; e.g., from secure mode to access mode (if the status of the network is changed, the alarm system operator must be advised of the mode change).

n.   Be performance-tested in accordance with established performance assurance procedures at a documented frequency (see DOE M 470.4-1).

3.   <u>RISK ASSESSMENT</u>. If conducted, a risk assessment must be documented. The conclusion must be that no risk exists or the risk is acceptable and in the best interests of the Government to accept it (based on a decision by the cognizant security authority).

CHAPTER A-V. PROTECTION DURING TRANSPORTATION

1. GENERAL REQUIREMENTS. This chapter defines requirements for the transportation of Category III and IV SNM. Category III quantities of SNM may be transported by the following methods unless otherwise prohibited by statute (see DOE O 460.2A, *Departmental Materials Transportation and Packaging Management*, dated 12-22-04). Other items of special national security interests may, on occasion, be designated for transportation safeguards system transport (see DOE O 461.1A, *Packaging and Transfer or Transportation of Materials of National Security Interest*, dated 4-26-04). Classified nuclear explosive parts, components, special assemblies, sub-critical test devices, trainers or shapes containing no fissile nuclear material or less than Category II quantities of fissile nuclear material must be shipped consistent with both DOE policy governing protection of classified information and Department of Transportation regulations governing interstate transportation.

2. CATEGORY III QUANTITIES OF SNM. Offsite shipments of Category III quantities of SNM may be transported by the following authorized methods unless otherwise prohibited by statute (see DOE O 460.2A).

    a. Domestic offsite shipments of classified configurations of Category III quantities of SNM must be made by Office of Secure Transportation (OST) or by an OST-approved commercial carrier that meets the requirements listed in paragraph 2b(1) below.

    b. Offsite shipments of unclassified configurations of Category III quantities of SNM are not required to be made by OST. If OST is not used, the shipments may be made by the following means:

        (1) Truck or Train Shipment. The following requirements must be met.Government-owned or exclusive-use truck, commercial carrier, or rail may be used.

            (b) Transport vehicles must be inspected by security personnel before loading and shipment. Cargo compartments must be locked and sealed after the inspection and remain sealed while en route.

            (c) Shipment escorts must periodically communicate with a control station operator. The control station operator must be capable of requesting appropriate local law enforcement agency response if needed.

            (d) No intermediate stops are permitted except for security interests.

        (2) Air Shipment. Shipments must be under the direct observation of the authorized escorts during all land movements and loading and unloading operations.

c.   Movement between security areas at the same site must comply with the locally developed and approved shipment security plan.

3.   <u>CATEGORY IV QUANTITIES OF SNM</u>. Category IV quantities of SNM may be transported by the following methods unless otherwise prohibited by statute.

a.   Domestic offsite shipments of classified configurations of Category IV quantities of SNM may be made by the OST or by other means when approved by DOE line management.

b.   Shipments of unclassified Category IV quantities of SNM may be made by truck, rail, air, or water craft in commercial for-hire or leased vehicles. Shippers are required to give the consignee an estimated time of arrival before dispatch and to follow-up with a written confirmation not later than 48 hours after dispatch.

c.   Consignees must promptly notify the shipper by telephone and written confirmation upon determination that a shipment has not arrived by the scheduled time. Upon initial notification, the shipper must report (see DOE M 470.4-1).

d.   Shipments must be made by a mode of transportation that can be traced, and within 24 hours from request, can report on the last known location of the shipment should it fail to arrive on schedule.

APPENDIX B. PROTECTION OF NUCLEAR WEAPONS, COMPONENTS, AND CATEGORY I AND II SPECIAL NUCLEAR MATERIAL

This appendix contains the physical protection requirements for Category I and II quantities of special nuclear material. These requirements are in addition to those physical protection requirements outlined in the base Manual and Appendix A.

CHAPTER B-I. PROTECTION OF NUCLEAR WEAPONS, COMPONENTS, AND CATEGORY I AND II SPECIAL NUCLEAR MATERIAL

1. GENERAL REQUIREMENTS. This chapter defines requirements for protecting nuclear weapons, components, and Category I and II quantities of SNM. The priority of protection measures must be designed to prevent malevolent acts such as theft, diversion, and radiological sabotage and to respond to adverse conditions such as emergencies caused by acts of nature. SNM must be protected at the higher level when roll-up to Category I quantities can occur within a single security area unless the facility has conducted an analysis that determined roll up was not credible. The policy cited in this chapter applies to fixed facilities and sites within a designated Protected Area (PA) or Material Access Area (MAA) and not the conduct of onsite movement of SNM or operations managed by the Office of Secure Transportation (OST). The OST is responsible for the promulgation of specific internal guidance governing the protection afforded all DOE matter entrusted to OST for transport by surface and air. Transportation of SNM, whether onsite or by OST, must be provided protection equivalent to that provided by fixed sites for the same material.

    a. A facility must not possess, receive, process, transport, or store nuclear weapons or SNM until that facility has been cleared (see DOE M 470.4-1, *Safeguards and Security Program Planning and Management*, dated 8-26-05).

    b. An integrated system of positive measures must be developed and implemented to protect Category I and II quantities of SNM and nuclear weapons. Protection measures must address physical protection strategies of denial and containment as well as recapture, recovery, and/or pursuit.

    c. Physical protection for each category of SNM must consider the following factors: quantities, chemical forms, and isotopic composition purities; ease of separation, accessibility, concealment, portability; radioactivity; and self-protecting features (see DOE M 470.4-6 Chg 1, and 10 CFR Part 73, Physical Protection of Plants and Materials, relative to self-protecting).

    d. The protection of nuclear material production, reactors, and fuel must be commensurate with the category of SNM.

    e. SNM, parts, explosives or munitions that are classified must receive the physical protection required by the highest level of classification or category of SNM, whichever is the more stringent.

2. CATEGORY I QUANTITIES OF SNM.

    a. In Use or Processing. Category I quantities of SNM must be located within a material access area (MAA) inside a protected area (PA). Any MAA containing unattended Category I quantities of SNM must be equipped with an intrusion detection system or detection must be provided by protective force.

b. Storage. Category I quantities of SNM must be stored within an MAA.

    (1) Category I, attractiveness level A SNM must be stored in a vault. Storage facilities constructed after July 15, 1994 for Category I, attractiveness level A SNM must be underground or below grade.

    (2) Category I, attractiveness level B SNM must be stored in a vault or provided enhanced protection that exceeds vault-type room (VTR) storage (e.g., collocated with a protective force response station and/or activated barriers).

    (3) At a minimum Category I, attractiveness level C SNM must be stored in a VTR.

3. CATEGORY II QUANTITIES OF SNM.

a. In Use or Processing. Category II quantities of SNM must be located within a PA and under material surveillance procedures.

b. Storage. Category II quantities of SNM must be stored in a vault or VTR located within a PA.

4. PROTECTED AREAS. PAs are security areas typically located within an LA that are established to protect Category II or greater quantities of SNM and may also contain classified matter. The PA provides concentric layers of security for the MAA. In addition to meeting LA requirements, the following apply to a PA.

a. General Requirements. PAs must be encompassed by physical barriers that identify the boundaries, surrounded by a perimeter intrusion detection and assessment system (PIDAS), and equipped with access controls that ensure only authorized personnel are allowed to enter and exit.

b. Inspection Program. An inspection program must ensure prohibited and controlled articles are detected before being brought into PA facilities. All personnel, vehicles, packages, and hand-carried articles are subject to inspection before entry into a security area. Likewise, such programs must ensure S&S interests are not removed. An inspection program must be established by the cognizant security authority and documented in the SSP.

c. Access Control. When the PIN or biometric system is either not working or not implemented at security areas requiring measures in addition to access control (e.g., at a PA or MAA boundary), PF or other trained security personnel must perform the access control requirements as documented in the SSP.

d. Personnel Access.

    (1) Unescorted access must be controlled to limit entry to individuals with an L or Q security clearance.

(a)   Visitor logs must be used for PAs.

(b)   Validation of the security clearance must occur at PA entry control points.

    <u>1</u>   The identity and security clearance of each person seeking entry must be validated by armed PF personnel or

    <u>2</u>   If PA access is controlled by an unattended automated access control system, the system must verify the following:

        <u>a</u>   a valid DOE security badge (badge validation must match the data assigned to the badge holder),

        <u>b</u>   valid security clearance, and

        <u>c</u>   valid PIN or

        <u>d</u>   valid biometric.

(2)   Vehicle Access.

(a)   Private vehicles are prohibited.

(b)   Government-owned or -leased vehicles may be admitted only when on official business and only when operated by properly cleared and authorized drivers or when the drivers are escorted by properly cleared and authorized personnel.

(c)   Vendor vehicles are prohibited unless the vehicles and drivers have been subjected to a thorough inspection/investigation and been given access approval by the DOE cognizant security authority. As an alternative, provisions must be established for using trained escorts.

(3)   Entrance Inspections. Entrance inspections of all personnel, vehicles, packages, and hand-carried items must be performed to deter and detect prohibited and controlled articles.

(a)   Bypass routes around inspection equipment must be closed or monitored to deter unauthorized passage of personnel and hand-carried articles.

(b)   Uninterrupted power must be provided to all control point inspection equipment.

(c)   Measures must be taken to preclude the unauthorized alteration of control settings on all entry/exit control point inspection equipment.

(d)   Equipment, to include portal monitors, must have both audible and visual alarms monitored by assigned PF personnel.

(e)   Ingress/egress points must be designed to preclude commingling of searched and unsearched personnel.

(f)   Passage of individuals, vehicles, and/or packages or mail through entry control point inspection equipment must be observed and controlled by PF personnel. Inspection equipment can include metal detectors, SNM detectors, explosive detectors, and x-ray systems and must ensure that prohibited and controlled articles specific for the PA are detected before being brought into DOE facilities. Hand-held and/or portable detectors, etc., must be available to resolve alarms and be available for use during inspection equipment failures.

(4)   Explosive Detection.

(a)   Sites must analyze their facilities to determine the potential for an adversary to use explosives to affect consequences and show that sufficient protective measures have been implemented to reduce the risk of a successful attack. The specific location of the screening will be determined by the cognizant security authority. In any instance it must be before gaining access to a PA. The scope of the protective measures are described in Chapter II of the base manual and supported by a risk analysis (see DOE M 470.4-1).

(b)   If the analysis determines that explosive detection is required, explosive detection equipment must ensure that explosives are not introduced without appropriate authorization. The SSP must document the analysis that establishes a facility's capability to detect explosives and provides protection against the malicious use of explosives.

(c)   Documentation must include the rationale for explosive detection equipment/systems selection, deployment, and use.

(5)   Metal Detection must be used in the entry process at all designated protected area boundaries.

(a)   Metal detectors must ensure prohibited and controlled articles are not introduced to designated protection areas without authorization.

(b)   Metal detectors used for entry inspection must detect test weapons listed in Chapter V.

(c)   Metal detectors scheduled to be replaced after Fiscal Year 2010 must meet the performance testing procedures and objects cited in Section 5.1, 5.2 and portions of 5.3 relating to non-ferro-magnetic stainless knives cited in National Institute of Justice (NIJ) Standard 0601.02, *Law Enforcement and Corrections Standards and Testing Program* (see Chapter X).

(6)   SNM Detectors. SNM detectors used in the inspection process must ensure SNM is not removed without authorization. The testing should provide for the identification of detection thresholds for the SNM type, form, quantity, attractiveness level, size, configuration, portability, and credible diversion amounts of articles or property contained within the area.

(7)   Exit Inspections. Personnel, vehicles, and hand-carried items including packages, briefcases, purses, and lunch containers are to be inspected to deter and detect unauthorized removal of classified matter or other S&S interests from PAs. The cognizant security authority is to determine whether the inspections will be conducted at the PA or MAA. The determination will be documented in a SSP.

(a)   SNM detectors and metal detectors must be used in a combination that precludes the opportunity to defeat the detectors individually and/or when used to inspect personnel for prohibited and controlled articles.

(b)   Metal detectors used in the exit inspection process must ensure shielded SNM is not removed without authorization.

(c)   Specific inspection procedures and the approach to responding to alarms with limitations and thresholds for SNM detectors must be established and documented in the SSP or a procedure.

(d)   Exit inspection procedures must be written to ensure the following.

1   Identification of detection thresholds for security interests. The thresholds must be consistent with the type, form, quantity, attractiveness level, size, configuration, portability, and credible diversion amounts of articles or property contained within the area.

2   The detection of shielded SNM (e.g., by using entry control point screening system equipment in a combination that

precludes the opportunity to defeat the detectors individually).

<u>3</u>   Entry control points without the means to detect unauthorized removal of material are not used to exit except in emergencies where equivalent protection measures are implemented when emergency exits are used (e.g., searches are conducted at an assembly area).

<u>4</u>   Random exit inspections are conducted at facility boundaries. The frequency must be determined by DOE line management.

(8)   Entry and Exit Control Points. Entry control point systems must allow the authorized entry and exit of personnel while detecting prohibited and controlled articles. Entry control point design must include separate material package inspection stations for inspecting personnel, packages, and hand-carried items. The following design criteria apply.

(a)   Entry/exit point inspection monitors must be collocated with PF posts to facilitate the initiation of a response to an alarm.

(b)   Security posts must be designed with an unobstructed view to facilitate observation of any attempt to bypass systems.

(c)   Security structures must meet the requirements in Appendix B, Chapter VII.

(d)   Entrances/exits must be equipped with intrusion detection sensors or controlled at all times.

5.   <u>MATERIAL ACCESS AREAS</u>. MAAs are security areas that are established to protect Category I quantities of SNM. In addition to requirements for a PA the following apply to an MAA.

a.   <u>General Requirements</u>. MAAs must have defined boundaries with barriers that provide sufficient delay time to impede, control, or deter unauthorized access.

(1)   MAAs must be located within a PA and must have distinct boundaries. Multiple MAAs may exist within a single PA; however, an MAA cannot cross a PA boundary.

(2)   While an MAA is required for the protection of Category I quantities of SNM, classified matter may exist within an MAA. In such instances, the classified matter must be stored according to the requirements in DOE M 470.4-4A.

b. <u>Access Control</u>. Access control must be administered by armed PF personnel and/or automated access control systems.

(1) Access must be controlled to limit entry to individuals with a Q security clearance and who have been authorized for entry consistent with need-to-know and operations.

(2) Individuals without appropriate security clearance must be escorted.

(a) The cognizant security authority must establish escort-to-visitor ratios for the MAA.

(b) The escort must ensure measures are taken to prevent compromise of classified matter or access to SNM.

(3) S&S interests, not in approved storage within an MAA, must be controlled by the custodian or authorized user.

(4) Validation of security clearance must occur at MAA entry control points.

(a) If MAA access is controlled by an unattended automated access control system, the system must verify:

<u>1</u>   a valid DOE security badge (badge validation must match the data assigned to the badge holder),

<u>2</u>   valid security clearance,

<u>3</u>   valid PIN, and

<u>4</u>   valid biometric template.

(b) The identity and security clearance of each person seeking entry may be validated by armed PF personnel or biometrics.

(5) Site-specific requirements and procedures for visitors must be developed and approved by DOE line management. The procedures must provide for the information described in Chapter II and Attachment 2.

c. <u>Entry/Exit Control Inspections</u>. Security requirements for entry/exit inspections must be established by DOE line management and documented in the SSP.

(1) A separate physical or electronic inspection of each vehicle, person, package, and container must be conducted at all MAA exit points.

(2) Metal detectors used for MAA entry inspection must detect the test weapons listed in Chapter V.

CHAPTER B-II. ALARM MANAGEMENT AND CONTROL SYSTEM

1. GENERAL REQUIREMENTS. The requirements for safeguards and security (S&S) alarm management and control systems used in the protection of Category I and II quantities of SNM and installed and operational after January 1, 2008, are contained in Appendix D of this Manual. This chapter establishes requirements for integrated physical protection systems protecting nuclear weapons, components, and category I and II SNM. Facilities with Category I and II quantities of SNM, or other high-consequence targets as identified by vulnerability assessments, must have a central alarm station (CAS) and a secondary alarm station (SAS). All intrusion detection system (IDS) sensors must annunciate directly to CAS/SAS when an alarm point is activated. Systems installed after July 15, 1994, must, where feasible, use redundant, independently routed, or separate communication paths to avoid a single-point failure. The perimeter intrusion detection and assessment system (PIDAS) surrounding the PA must be monitored in a continuously manned CAS and SAS. In addition to the requirements in Appendix A for Category III and IV SNM, the following requirements apply.

    a. Central Alarm Station.

        (1) The CAS must be attended continually.

        (2) The CAS and SAS must be physically separated.

        (3) To avoid a single-point failure, systems for the protection of Category I and II quantities of SNM installed after July 15, 1994, must, where feasible, use redundant, independently routed, or separate communication paths.

        (4) The CAS must be designed as a hardened post, located within a limited area (LA) or greater security area and manned 24 hours a day.

        (5) Exterior walls, windows, doors, and roofs must be constructed of, or reinforced with, materials that have a bullet-penetration resistance equivalent to the Level 8 rating given in Underwriters Laboratories (UL) Standard 752, *Standard for Bullet-Resisting Equipment*.

        (6) Entryways must be fitted with doors equipped with locks that can be operated from within the alarm station.

    b. Secondary Alarm Station. The SAS must be used as an alternative alarm annunciation point to the CAS and be manned 24 hours a day so that a response can be initiated if the CAS cannot perform its intended function.

        (1) The SAS need not be fully redundant to the CAS but must be capable of providing full command and control in response to S&S events [see paragraph 1a(3) above].

        (2) The SAS may be located in a property protection area.

2.   <u>CLOSED-CIRCUIT TELEVISION (CCTV) SYSTEM</u>. CCTV assessment systems must be functional under day, night, overcast, and artificial lighting conditions. The system must provide a clear and suitable image for assessment.

   a.   <u>Primary Assessment</u>. When used as the primary means of alarm assessment and to determine response level, the system requirements are listed below.

      (1)   CCTV systems must annunciate when the video signal from the camera is disrupted or lost.

      (2)   The video subsystem must be integrated with the CAS/SAS alarm display systems.

      (3)   The system must have the capability to automatically switch to the camera associated with the alarm event and to display that event for operator assessment.

      (4)   Video recorders must be actuated by the intrusion alarm and record automatically.

      (5)   Video recorder response time must be rapid enough to record the actual intrusion, be able to capture sufficient information for alarm assessment, and have the capacity to store at least 45 days of "event logs" before archiving the information to removable nonvolatile media.

      (6)   Video assessment coverage must be complete (e.g., no gaps between zones or areas that cannot be assessed because of shadows or objects blocking the camera's field of view).

      (7)   CCTV used for primary assessment must be tamper protected on a 24 hour circuit (camera enclosures and the video and data lines) and use fixed cameras with fixed focal length lenses that provide a clear image for assessment (pan tilt and zoom cameras may be used for surveillance).

      (8)   CCTV systems must use real-time signal or near real-time transmission of camera views.

      (9)   The video system must accept manual override of automatic features. This capability permits the operation of a CCTV camera associated with another event.

   b.   <u>Additional CCTV Requirements</u>.

      (1)   When CCTV systems are used, the alarm control system must be able to call the operators' attention to an alarm associated video recorder/monitor.

      (2)   The video assessment must be supported by sufficient lighting or other means necessary to facilitate alarm assessment.

(3)   The picture quality must allow the operator to recognize and discriminate between human and animal presence in the camera field of view.

CHAPTER B-III. COMMUNICATIONS, ELECTRICAL POWER, AND LIGHTING

1.   COMMUNICATIONS.

    a.   General Requirements. Communications equipment must meet the following requirements.

        (1)   Redundant Voice Communications. Facilities protecting Category I and II quantities of SNM must have a minimum of two different voice communications technologies to link the CAS/SAS to each fixed post and protective force (PF) duty location. Alternative communications capabilities must be available immediately if the primary communications system fails. Channels considered critical to protective personnel communications must have backup channels.

        (2)   Records. Records of the failure and repair of all PF radio communications equipment must be maintained so that type of failure, unit serial number, and equipment type can be compiled.

        (3)   Recording of Communication. A continuous electronic recording system must be provided for all security radio traffic and telecommunications that provide support to the CAS. The recorder must be equipped with a time track and must cover all security channels. Sites must follow the established requirements for consensual Listening-In to or Recording Telephone/Radio Conversations as contained in DOE 1450.4, *Consensual Listening-in to or Recording Telephone/Radio Conversations*, dated 11-12-92.

    b.   Communication Systems. Protection system communications must support two vital functions: alarm communication/display and PF communications. PF communications include the procedures and hardware that enable officers to communicate with each other.

        (1)   Design Considerations. The design of a PF communication system must address resistance to eavesdropping, vulnerability to transmission of deceptive messages, and susceptibility to jamming.

        (2)   Protective Force Radio System Requirements. The application of digital encryption may be implemented on a graded basis. When the PF communications are converted to meet Federal Communications Commission (FCC) narrow band frequency requirements, digital encryption (see ANSI/TIA/EIA-102 Phase I, referred to as Project 25) must be included.

        (3)   Alternative Means of Communication. Alternative means of communication must be in place such as telephones, intercoms, public

address systems, hand signals, sirens, lights, pagers, couriers, computer terminals, flares, duress alarms, smoke, or whistles.

(4)   Local Law Enforcement Agency (LLEA) Communication. A mechanism must be established to ensure communication with LLEAs. An alternative communications capability from a SAS must be provided if the primary station is compromised. Daily tests of these communications systems must be conducted with LLEAs unless a different rate is required by memorandum of agreement/understanding and is documented in the site security plan (SSP).

c.   Duress Systems. Facilities with protected areas and material access areas must have duress notification capabilities for mobile and fixed posts and for the CAS/SAS. The duress system must meet the following requirements.

(1)   Activation of the duress alarm must be as unobtrusive as practicable. The duress alarm must annunciate at the CAS and SAS but not at the initiating PF post.

(2)   The duress alarm for a CAS must annunciate at the SAS while the duress alarm for the SAS must annunciate at the CAS.

(3)   Mobile duress alarms must annunciate at the CAS, SAS, or another fixed post.

(4)   All PF fixed posts must have duress devices (see DOE M 470.4-3A, *Contractor Protective Force*, dated 11-5-08).

d.   Radios. Fixed-post radios, mobile radios, and portable radios must be provided to support operational security requirements.

(1)   Radio System Requirements. The radio system must be capable of accessing security operational and support channels.

(a)   Radios must have power and sensitivity for two-way voice communications with the facility base stations using the primary channel.

(b)   Security communication channels must be restricted to security operations.

(c)   Radio system components must be protected against destruction and unauthorized access.

(d)   Radio programming consoles must be protected from unauthorized programming changes.

(e)   Radio systems components must be protected from physical damage.

(2)   Portable Radios. Portable radios must be capable of two-way communication on the primary security channel from within buildings and structures. An alternative means of communications must be provided if safety or process procedures prohibit transmission within a building or structure.

(3)   Two-Way Communications. Mobile radios and base station radios must be capable of maintaining two-way communication with the CAS/SAS on the primary channel.

(4)   Emergency Response Channels. Base stations, which are controlled from the CAS, must include emergency response channels.

(5)   Battery Power. Portable radios must operate for an 8-hour period at maximum expected duty cycles. Procedures for radio exchange, battery exchange, or battery recharges can be used to meet this requirement.

(6)   Repeater Stations. A radio repeater station must be placed in a location that ensures all-weather access for vehicles and personnel to the station building, antenna, standby generator plant, and fuel storage tanks. The station must be designed to minimize risk of damage to the antenna structure and supporting guide lines from vehicular traffic.

e.   PF Tracking Systems. Systems capable of tracking and displaying the live movements and state-of-health of PF may be used to improve the situational awareness of PF commanders. Data associated with these systems are typically transmitted by radio frequency so the following limitations apply:

(1)   Classified information may not be transmitted by the wireless communications associated with tracking systems.

(2)   PF tracking systems used at sites with Category I quantities of SNM must be evaluated prior to implementation by the cognizant security authority. The evaluation is to determine if the high system effectiveness rating, as described in DOE M 470.4-1, would be degraded, if compromised unless encrypted.

f.   Radio Frequency Alarm Communications. The radio frequency alarm communications systems, when used to protect Category I and II quantities of SNM, must be limited to emergency, temporary situations, or early warning detection applications. When used, a comprehensive risk assessment must be conducted and a DOE Graded Security Protection (GSP) implementation plan established. Radio frequency alarm systems and associated communication systems used for the protection of Category I and II quantities of SNM must comply with the requirements outlined for the protection of Category III and IV quantities of SNM and meet the following additional requirements.

(1)   RF alarm communications systems are used for auxiliary security applications and do not require the same robustness as primary systems for protection of Category I and II quantities of SNM.

(2)   Use of a RF alarm communications system must be evaluated prior to implementation by the cognizant security authority and determined to not effect a high system effectiveness rating as described in DOE M 470.4-1, if compromised.

2.   ELECTRICAL POWER.

a.   Primary Power Supply. All IDSs protecting S&S interests must have a primary power source from normal onsite power. Early warning systems that have self-contained electrical power are exempt from this requirement. Power sources must contain a switching capability for operational testing to determine required auxiliary power sources. The following power supply requirements apply:

b.   Alarm and Communication Systems. Normal primary power must come directly from the onsite power distribution system or for isolated facilities, directly from the public utility.

(1)   Communications and Automated Information Systems, Alarm Stations, and Radio Repeater Stations. Critical system elements must be connected to an uninterruptible power supply (UPS) or to auxiliary power.

(2)   Radio System Centers. Power supply requirements must be determined assuming that all transmitters are keyed simultaneously while associated receivers and other equipment and building services are in operation.

c.   Auxiliary Power Sources. Intrusion detection and assessment, automated access control, and CCTV systems protecting Category I and II quantities of SNM and/or Top Secret matter must have an auxiliary power capability.

(1)   Transfer to auxiliary power must be automatic upon failure of the primary source and must not affect operation of the protection system, subcomponents, or devices.

(2)   The CAS and SAS must receive an alarm indicating failure of the protection system's primary power and immediately transfer to the auxiliary power source.

(3)   When used, rechargeable batteries must be kept fully charged or subject to automatic recharging whenever the voltage drops to a level specified by the battery manufacturer. Non-rechargeable batteries must be replaced based on manufacturer's recommendations. The system must be capable

of generating a low-battery alarm which shall be transmitted to the CAS and SAS.

    (4)   Power sources must have the necessary built-in features to facilitate periodic operational testing to verify their readiness.

    d.   <u>Uninterruptible Power Sources</u>. UPS must be provided for systems requiring continuous power and considered for systems that, if interrupted, would degrade the protection of the associated security area.

3.   <u>LIGHTING</u>.

    a.   Lights must support a 24-hour visual assessment and provide, as a minimum, 2 foot-candle illumination at ground level for at least a 30-feet (9.14-meters) diameter around PF posts and a minimum of 0.2-foot candle illumination within the PIDAS isolation zone.

    b.   Sufficient lighting for assessment must be maintained on the PIDAS sensor zones and the clear zones for CCTV assessment and surveillance 24 hours a day. The lighting must compliment the CCTV system in supporting its video assessment capability.

    c.   Where protective lighting at remote locations is not feasible, PF patrols and/or fixed posts must be equipped with night-vision and/or thermal imaging devices. Night-vision and/or thermal imaging devices should not be used routinely in lieu of protective lighting at entrances and exits but may be used if lighting is lost.

    d.   Light glare must be minimized.

    e.   Light sources on protected perimeters must be located so that illumination is directed outward so that the PF is not blinded or silhouetted.

    f.   When back-up emergency lighting is used, it must be periodically tested to ensure that it will function as configured for a specified sustained period.

CHAPTER B-IV. INTRUSION DETECTION AND ASSESSMENT SYSTEMS

1. GENERAL REQUIREMENTS. Nuclear weapons and Category I and II quantities of SNM must be protected by an integrated physical protection system using protective force, barriers, and Intrusion Detection and Assessment Systems (IDAS).

   a. Protecting SNM. The following requirements apply for alarms protecting Category I and II quantities of SNM.

      (1) Interior or exterior Intrusion Detection and Assessment Systems (IDASs) must be designed with independent, redundant data communication lines.

      (2) Intrusion detection and assessment must be immediate.

      (3) The video signal must be protected based on the classification level. Video signal protection would include video signal encryption for conditions wherein video coverage cannot be masked from viewing classified matter.

   b. Early Warning Intrusion Detection. Sites may use early warning intrusion detection to supplement their PIDAS as a means of achieving increased adversary detection and improved overall system performance. The false and nuisance alarm rates, degradation, and detection area maintenance requirements of a PIDAS do not apply to early warning systems. Each individual early warning or extended range exterior intrusion detection sensor must have false and nuisance alarm rates that do not degrade the overall effectiveness of the system, including monitoring personnel's ability to assess and manage alarms, and be documented in the site security plan (SSP).

2. EXTERIOR INTRUSION DETECTION SYSTEM. Exterior IDASs are designed to detect unauthorized entry into security areas.

   a. Exterior IDS. The location of communication lines must be documented in the SSP consistent with Table 1, Line Supervision Protection (see Chapter IX of the base Manual).

      (1) Intrusion detection and assessment systems must function effectively in all environmental conditions and under all types of lighting conditions or compensatory measures must be implemented.

      (2) PIDAS must use multilayered, complementary intrusion detection sensors.

   b. Detection Capability. A PIDAS must be capable of detecting an individual crossing the detection zone by walking, crawling, jumping, running, rolling, or climbing the fence at any point in the detection zone, with a detection probability of 90 percent and confidence level of 95 percent. Performance testing should be conducted to determine the proper settings for high detection rates with the lowest possible nuisance alarm rates. Tests should be performed with a low-profile target (crawling) and a higher velocity and profile targets (walking, running, fast-crawl, rolling). Whenever practical, the tests should be conducted under the sort of adverse weather and lighting conditions that are common to the local environment.

(1)   The IDS must be tested when installed and annually (at least every 12 months) thereafter to validate that it meets detection probability and confidence level requirements.

(2)   Any time the IDS falls below the required probability of detection, the IDS must be repaired and retested.

(3)   When calculating detection probability for multiple sensor systems, detection is assumed if any of the sensors report an intrusion.

(4)   Additional operability and effectiveness testing must be conducted and documented in the SSP (see DOE M 470.4-1).

c.   Perimeter Intrusion Detection and Assessment System. The PIDAS surrounding the protected area must be monitored in a continuously manned central alarm station and a secondary alarm station. PIDAS must be:

(1)   designed to cover the entire perimeter without a gap in detection, including the walls and roofs of structures situated within the designated security area;

(2)   located such that the length of each detection zone is consistent with the characteristics of the sensors used in that zone and the topography;

(3)   designed, installed, and maintained to prevent adversaries from circumventing the detection system;

(4)   systems installed after July 15, 1994, must, where economically feasible, use redundant, independently routed, or separate communication paths, to avoid a single-point failure;

(5)   provided with an isolation zone at least 20-feet (6-meters) wide and clear of fabricated or natural objects that would interfere with operation of detection systems or the effectiveness of the assessment; and

(6)   free of wires, piping, poles, and similar objects that could be used to assist an intruder traversing the isolation zone or that could assist in the undetected ingress or egress of an adversary or matter.

d.   PIDAS Zone Degradation. Each PIDAS detection zone must be kept free of snow, ice, grass, weeds, debris, wildlife, and any other item that may degrade the effectiveness of the system. When this cannot be accomplished and detection capabilities become degraded, compensatory measures must be taken.

e.   <u>Preventive Maintenance</u>. PIDAS, security area and other security lighting, and security system-related emergency power or auxiliary power supplies must be included in a preventive maintenance program.

CHAPTER B-V. ACCESS CONTROLS AND ENTRY/EXIT INSPECTIONS

1. <u>ACCESS CONTROL SYSTEMS AND ENTRY CONTROL POINTS</u>. Entry control points must be located within the PIDAS and protected by the PIDAS when not in use. This configuration must provide a continuous PIDAS zone at the barrier that encompasses the entry control point. The entry control point should permit entry of only one person at a time into PAs and MAAs. Electronic entry control point search equipment (e.g., metal detectors) must annunciate locally to a protective force-staffed entry control point instead of annunciating at the CAS and SAS.

2. <u>AUTOMATED ACCESS CONTROL SYSTEMS</u>. Automated access control systems may be used in place of or in conjunction with protective or other authorized personnel to meet access requirements.

   a. Both the CAS and SAS must monitor the automated access control system's intrusion alarm events.

   b. Badge readers at PAs and MAAs must have anti-passback protection.

3. <u>ENTRY/EXIT INSPECTIONS</u>. Entry/exit inspections are required at PAs and MAAs, and at other security areas as required by DOE line management and documented in the SSP.

   a. Entry inspections of personnel, hand-carried items, packages, and/or vehicles must ensure prohibited articles are detected and are not introduced without authorization.

   b. Exit inspections must ensure S&S interests are not removed without authorization.

4. <u>EMERGENCY PERSONNEL AND VEHICLES</u>. Emergency personnel and vehicles may be authorized for immediate entry to security areas in response to an emergency if:

   a. The protective force (PF) or other designated site personnel maintain continuous surveillance of all emergency vehicles that enter the site.

   b. Arrangements must be made to inspect emergency personnel and vehicles when exiting after the emergency is over or when leaving the site. If the emergency condition prevents an exit inspection before departing the site, an escort must be provided, and both personnel and emergency vehicles must be inspected as soon as the emergency is over.

CHAPTER B-VI. SECURE STORAGE

1. <u>SPECIAL NUCLEAR MATERIAL VAULT</u>. An SNM vault must be a penetration-resistant enclosure that has doors, walls, floor, and roof/ceiling designed and constructed to significantly delay penetration from forced entry and equipped with intrusion detection system devices on openings allowing access. The material thickness must be determined by the requirement for forcible entry delay times for the safeguards and security interests stored within, but must not be less than the delay time provided by a minimum 8-inch (20.32-centimeters)-thick reinforced concrete poured in place with a 28-day compressive strength of 2,500 pounds per square inch (17,237 kilopascal). Activated technologies such as activated barriers or passive/active denial systems may be used in lieu of thicker concrete when analysis indicates that delay times exceeding that of 8-inch (20.32-centimeters)-thick reinforced concrete are required. The site's analysis of the protection measures in use must be documented in the site security plan.

2. <u>VAULT DOOR</u>. A vault door and frame must meet the General Services Administration's (GSA's) highest level of penetration resistance. The lock on the door must be a minimum of a GSA-approved Federal Supply Schedule-listed high-security lock, as described in Chapter IV of the base Manual.

3. <u>WALL PENETRATIONS</u>. Any openings of a size and shape to permit unauthorized entry (larger than 96 square inches [619.2 square centimeters] in area and more than 6 inches [15.24 centimeters] in its smallest dimension) must be equipped with the measures described in Chapter VIII of this Manual.

CHAPTER B-VII. PROTECTIVE FORCE POSTS

1. <u>PROTECTIVE FORCE POSTS</u>.

    a. <u>Special Nuclear Material Access</u>. Permanent PF posts controlling access to protected areas and material access areas must be constructed to meet the requirements for a hardened post. Exterior walls, windows, roofs, and doors must be constructed of, or reinforced with, materials that have a bullet-penetration resistance equivalent to the Level 8 high-power rifle rating given in Underwriters Laboratory (UL) *Standard for <u>Bullet Resisting Equipment</u>*.

    b. <u>PF Towers</u>. PF towers intended to be used as tactical fighting positions must have, as a minimum, a bullet-penetration resistance equivalent to the Level 8 high-power rifle rating given in UL-752, *Standard for <u>Bullet Resisting Equipment</u>*.

    c. <u>Fighting Positions</u>. Designated fighting positions must be sited in locations that command significant fields of fire and must be able to serve as bases of maneuver for PF tactical units. These positions must, as a minimum, have a bullet-penetration resistance equivalent to .50 caliber armor piercing.

2. <u>RESPONSE CAPABILITY</u>. A response capability will be used to deny, neutralize, contain, and/or perform recapture/recovery and pursuit missions within the required timelines (see DOE M 470.4-3 Chg 1 and/or DOE M 470.4-3A).

CHAPTER B-VIII. BARRIERS

1. <u>GENERAL REQUIREMENTS.</u>

    a. Barriers must be used to facilitate effective, economical use of protective personnel while maximizing their tactical posture.

    b. Barriers must be used to direct the flow of personnel and vehicular traffic through designated entry control points to permit efficient operation of access controls and entry point inspections and to provide PFs the ability to identify and engage adversaries along all feasible pathways.

    c. A clear zone must be provided along each side of security fences to facilitate intrusion detection and assessment. Double fences should be separated by a clear zone of at least 20 feet (6 m).

    d. The barrier design must deter or prevent an insider from diverting S&S interests past the barrier for retrieval.

2. <u>PENETRATION OF SECURITY AREA BARRIERS.</u> In addition to the requirements for a limited area, penetration of security area barrier requirements for a PA includes the following:

    a. Overhead utilities must not allow for access into a PA or higher security area without physical protection features to prevent or detect unauthorized access into the security area.

    b. Two permanent, continuous parallel fences (requirement for the perimeter intrusion detection and assessment system) must identify the boundary of the PA.

    c. Barrier requirements for a material access area include those required for a PA in addition to the following:

        (1) Barriers must delay or deter the unauthorized movement of SNM while allowing access by authorized personnel and material movement through entry control points and emergency evacuation as necessary.

        (2) Doors at entry control points such as transfer locations must be alarmed, and the alarms must communicate with the central alarm station/ secondary alarm station when an unauthorized exit occurs.

        (3) PF response time to an intrusion alarm must be less than the delay time that can be demonstrated from the time an alarm is activated at the PA boundary until the task is completed.

        (4) Penetrations in the floors, walls, or ceilings for piping, heating, venting, air conditioning, or other support systems must not create accessible paths that could facilitate the removal or diversion of S&S interests. Exits

designed for emergency evacuation must be alarmed with an intrusion detection system or controlled at all times.

3.   BARRIERS-DELAY MECHANISMS. Mechanisms must be used to deter and delay access, removal, or unauthorized use of Category I and II quantities of SNM and nuclear weapons.

   a.   Delay mechanisms may include both passive physical barriers (e.g., walls, ceilings, floors, windows, doors, and security bars) and activated barriers (e.g., sticky foam, pop-up barriers, cold smoke and high-intensity sound). The appropriate delay mechanisms must be used at site-specified target locations to reduce reliance on PF recapture/recovery operations.

   b.   Active and passive denial systems will be deployed, as appropriate, to reduce reliance on recapture operations.

4.   ACTIVATED BARRIERS, DETERRENTS, AND OBSCURANTS. If used, activated barrier and deterrent systems must meet site-specific requirements when deployed at improvised nuclear device/radiological dispersal device denial target locations. Activated barriers, deterrents, and obscurants must meet the following requirements:

   a.   Obscurants must consider spatial density versus time to deploy as determined by vulnerability analysis.

   b.   Dispensable materials must be individually evaluated for effectiveness of delay.

   c.   Controls and dispensers must be protected from tampering and must not be collocated.

5.   VEHICLE BARRIERS. Vehicle barriers must be used to preclude, deter, and where necessary, prevent penetration into security areas when such access cannot otherwise be controlled.

   a.   At Category I/II facilities, all potential vehicle approach routes to identified target areas must have barriers installed that will preclude an adversary from reaching the target.

   b.   If required by vehicle barrier design limits, speed reducers must be used to slow adversary vehicles to achieve site-specific threat/target system response requirements.

   c.   These requirements must be consistent with the operation of the facility and protection goals as documented in the vulnerability analysis.

CHAPTER B-IX. PROTECTION DURING TRANSPORTATION

1.   GENERAL REQUIREMENTS. This chapter defines requirements for the transportation of Category I and II SNM. Packages or containers containing SNM must be sealed with tamper-indicating devices.

2.   OFFSITE SHIPMENT. Offsite shipment of fissile nuclear materials of national security interest Category I and II quantities of SNM must be transported within the Transportation Safeguards System as addressed in DOE O 460.2A, *Departmental Materials Transportation and Packaging Management*. Specific items included in this policy are nuclear explosives, nuclear explosive components, special assemblies, sub-critical test devices, trainers, bulk fissile nuclear materials, and truck-transported naval fuel elements.

3.   ONSITE SHIPMENTS. Movements of SNM between protected areas at the same site or between protected areas and staging areas on the same site must be escorted by armed protective force officers.

CHAPTER B-X. MAINTENANCE

1. <u>MAINTENANCE</u>. Maintenance must be performed on site-determined critical and non-critical system elements.

    a. <u>Compensatory Measures</u>. Compensatory measures must be implemented immediately when any part of the critical system element protecting Category I and II quantities of SNM, is out of service. Compensatory measures must be continued until maintenance is complete and the critical system is back in service.

    b. <u>Corrective Maintenance within 24 Hours</u>. Corrective maintenance must be initiated within 24 hours of receiving a report that there has been a malfunction of a site-determined critical system element protecting Category I and II quantities of SNM.

    c. <u>Corrective Maintenance within 72 Hours</u>. Corrective maintenance must be initiated within 72 hours of detection of a malfunction for all other protection system elements protecting Category I and II SNM.

    d. <u>Non-Critical Systems Maintenance</u>. For non-critical system elements, the cognizant security authority must approve compensatory measure implementation procedures.

2. <u>PREVENTIVE MAINTENANCE</u>. Preventive maintenance must be performed on critical subsystems and components in accordance with manufacturers' specifications and/or local procedures.

3. <u>MAINTENANCE PERSONNEL SECURITY CLEARANCES</u>. Personnel who test, maintain, or service critical system elements must have security clearances consistent with the S&S interest being protected.

    a. Security clearances are not required when such testing and maintenance are performed as bench services away from the security area.

    b. Systems or critical system elements bench-tested or maintained away from the security area by personnel without the appropriate security clearances must be inspected and operationally tested by qualified and cleared personnel before being returned to service.

    c. Personnel who test, maintain, or service non-critical system elements must have security clearances consistent with the S&S interest being protected as determined by the cognizant security authority.

4. <u>TESTING AND MAINTENANCE OF SCREENING EQUIPMENT</u>. Screening equipment can include explosive detectors, metal detectors, x-ray systems, and SNM detectors and must ensure that prohibited and controlled articles are detected before being permitted into Department of Energy facilities.

a.   The following should be used as standard test weapons or the site must implement the performance testing procedures and test objects cited in Sections 5.1, 5.2 and the portion of 5.3 of NIJ Standard 0601.02, Law Enforcement and Corrections Standards and Testing Program, relating to non-ferromagnetic stainless steel knives:

    (1)   steel and aluminum alloy .25 caliber automatic pistol manufactured in Italy by Armi Tanfoglio Giuseppe, sold in the United States by Excam as Model GT27B and by F.I.E. the Titan (weight: about 343 grams); or

    (2)   aluminum, model 7, .380 caliber Derringer manufactured by American Derringer Corporation (weight: about 200 grams); and

    (3)   stainless steel 0.22 caliber long rifle mini-revolver, manufactured by North American Arms (weight: approximately 129 grams).

b.   X-ray machines may be used to supplement metal detectors and protective personnel hand searches for prohibited and controlled articles.

    (1)   X-ray machines must provide a discernable image of prohibited and controlled articles.

    (2)   X-ray machines must image an unobstructed (discernable) set of wires and other objects as described in American Society for Testing and Materials (ASTM) standard for test objects (see ASTM Standard F792-01e2, *Standard Practice for Evaluating the Imaging Performance of Security X-ray Systems*).

c.   SNM detectors used in the inspection process must be tested using trace elements that depict the type of material located within the security area. The testing should provide for the identification of detection thresholds for the prohibited/controlled articles. The thresholds must be consistent with the SNM type, form, quantity, attractiveness level, site, configuration, portability, and credible diversion amounts of articles or property contained within the area.

5.   <u>RECORD KEEPING</u>.

a.   Testing and maintenance records must be retained in accordance with the requirements of approved records management procedures.

b.   Records of the failure and repair of all communications equipment must be maintained so that type of failure, unit serial number, and equipment type can be compiled.

APPENDIX C. SAFEGUARDS AND SECURITY ALARM MANAGEMENT AND CONTROL SYSTEMS (SAMACS)

The requirements for Safeguards and Security Alarm Management and Control Systems used in protection of Category I and II quantities of special nuclear material and installed and operational after January 1, 2008, are provided in Appendix C, which contains unclassified controlled nuclear information and will be issued separately from this Manual. This document has not been revised since it was originally published on 8-26-05. A copy of Appendix C may be obtained by contacting the Office of Security Policy at 301-903-6209.

**CONTRACTOR REQUIREMENTS DOCUMENT
DOE M 470.4-2A, *PHYSICAL PROTECTION***

This contractor requirements document (CRD) establishes the requirements for DOE contractors whose contracts involve responsibilities for administering DOE Physical Security Programs for the purpose of protecting safeguards and security (S&S) interests.

Regardless of the performer of the work, the contractor is responsible for complying with the requirements of this CRD. The contractor is responsible for flowing down the requirements of this CRD to subcontractors at any tier to the extent necessary to ensure the contractor's compliance with the requirements.

TABLE OF CONTENTS

ATTACHMENT 1. CONTRACTOR REQUIREMENTS DOCUMENT DOE M 470.4-2A, *PHYSICAL PROTECTION* i

Chapter I . PROTECTION PLANNING I-1

Chapter II . SECURITY AREAS II-1

Chapter III . POSTING NOTICES III-1

Chapter IV . LOCKS AND KEYS IV-1

Chapter V . MAINTENANCE V-1

Chapter VI . BARRIERS VI-1

Chapter VII . COMMUNICATIONS, ELECTRICAL POWER AND LIGHTING VII-1

Chapter VIII . SECURE STORAGE VIII-1

Chapter IX . INTRUSION DETECTION AND ASSESSMENT SYSTEMS IX-1

Chapter X . ENTRY/EXIT SCREENING X-1

APPENDIX A. PROTECTION OF CATEGORY III AND IV SPECIAL NUCLEAR MATERIAL .... A-i

CHAPTER A-I. PROTECTION OF CATEGORY III AND IV SPECIAL NUCLEAR MATERIAL A-I-1

CHAPTER A-II. ALARM MANAGEMENT AND CONTROL SYSTEM A-II-1

CHAPTER A-III. INTRUSION DETECTION AND ASSESSMENT SYSTEMS A-III-1

CHAPTER A-IV. COMMUNICATIONS A-IV-1

CHAPTER A-V. PROTECTION DURING TRANSPORTATION A-V-1

APPENDIX B. PROTECTION OF NUCLEAR WEAPONS, COMPONENTS, AND CATEGORY I AND II SPECIAL NUCLEAR MATERIAL .... B-i

CHAPTER B-I. PROTECTION OF NUCLEAR WEAPONS, COMPONENTS, AND CATEGORY I AND II SPECIAL NUCLEAR MATERIAL B-I-1

CHAPTER B-II. ALARM MANAGEMENT AND CONTROL SYSTEM B-II-1

CHAPTER B-III. COMMUNICATIONS, ELECTRICAL POWER, AND LIGHTING B-III-1

CHAPTER B-IV. INTRUSION DETECTION AND ASSESSMENT SYSTEMS B-IV-1

CHAPTER B-V. ACCESS CONTROLS AND ENTRY/EXIT INSPECTIONS B-V-1

CHAPTER B-VI. SECURE STORAGE B-VI-1

CHAPTER B-VII. PROTECTIVE FORCE POSTS B-VII-1

CHAPTER B-VIII. BARRIERS B-VIII-1

CHAPTER B-IX. PROTECTION DURING TRANSPORTATION B-IX-1

APPENDIX C. SAFEGUARDS AND SECURITY ALARM MANAGEMENT AND CONTROL SYSTEMS (SAMACS) C-1

CHAPTER I. PROTECTION PLANNING

1. <u>GENERAL REQUIREMENTS</u>. This CRD establishes requirements for the physical protection of all Departmental interests including Departmental property and national S&S interests under DOE's purview. Interests requiring protection range from Government facilities, buildings, property and employees, to national security interests such as classified information, SNM and nuclear weapons. Radiological, chemical, or biological sabotage targets must be provided protection as determined by vulnerability analysis. Select biological agents and toxins are also considered DOE interests. Protection of these select biological agents and toxins are governed by Title 7 Code of Federal Regulations (CFR) Part 331, *Possession, Use, and Transfer of Select Agents and Toxins*; 9 CFR Part 121, *Possession, Use, and Transfer of Select Agents and Toxins*; 9 CFR Part 122, *Organisms and Vectors*; and 42 CFR Part 73, *Select Agents and Toxins*. Protection of chemical facilities/activities which are considered to present a high risk is governed by Title 6 CFR Part 27, *Chemical Facility Anti-Terrorism Standards; Final Rule*.

   a. Depending on the interest, protection may be required based on best business practices, economic rationale, national security objectives or other rationale.

   b. DOE line management considers the various Departmental interests and their attractiveness to theft, diversion or sabotage when developing protection requirements using graded protection fundamentals.

   c. Physical protection strategies must be developed, documented, and implemented consistent with the Graded Security Protection (GSP), formerly the Design Basis Threat Policy, and National policy to protect radiological, chemical, or biological sabotage (see DOE O 470.3B, *Graded Security Protection Policy*).

2. <u>PLANNING</u>. The implementation of graded physical protection programs required by this CRD must be systematically planned, executed, evaluated, and documented as described by a site security plan (see DOE M 470.4-1).

   a. Physical protection programs must be based on the most recent GSP information and used in conjunction with local threat guidance. The GSP applies to all DOE facilities including those that do not possess classified matter or SNM (see DOE O 470.3B).

   b. Departmental interests must be protected from malevolent acts such as theft, diversion, and sabotage and events such as natural disasters and civil disorder by considering site and regional threats, protection planning strategies, and protection measures.

   c. SNM must be protected at the higher level when roll-up to a higher category can occur within a single security area unless the facility has conducted an analysis that determined roll-up was not credible (see DOE M 470.4-6 Chg 1 and DOE M 470.4-7).

d. Sites upgrading security measures must consider the benefits provided using security technology by conducting life-cycle cost-benefit analyses comparing the effectiveness of security technology to traditional manpower-based methodologies. However, at Category I and Category II facilities various manpower alternatives to include security technologies must be used to allow protective force personnel to concentrate on the primary mission of protecting nuclear weapons, SNM, and designated high-value targets.

3. <u>PERFORMANCE ASSURANCE</u>. Physical protection systems, including components, must be performance tested to ensure overall system effectiveness. The effectiveness of physical protection systems and programs must be determined through performance testing at a frequency determined by the cognizant security authority and in accordance with the Performance Assurance Program. A program of scheduled testing and maintenance must be implemented to ensure an effective, fully functional security system (see DOE M 470.4-1).

4. <u>PHYSICAL PROTECTION SURVEILLANCE EQUIPMENT</u>. If physical protection surveillance equipment is to be used to support the facility's physical protection strategy, it must be identified and its physical protection application must be described in the site security plan. Procedures must be developed to prohibit misuse of physical protection surveillance equipment (e.g., video assessment and audio communication/recording equipment).

CHAPTER II. SECURITY AREAS

1. <u>GENERAL REQUIREMENTS</u>. Security areas are established to provide protection to a wide array of S&S interests under the Department's purview, to include nuclear weapons, SNM, classified information, buildings, facilities, Government property, employees and other interests. The security areas described in this Chapter address a graded approach for the protection of S&S interests.

2. <u>GENERAL ACCESS AREAS (GAAs)</u>. GAAs may be established to allow access to certain areas with minimum security requirements as determined by the cognizant security authority.

   a. <u>General Requirements</u>. These designated areas are accessible to all personnel including the public. DOE line management should establish security requirements for those areas designated as a GAA.

   b. <u>Posting of General Access Areas</u>. The designated GAA security requirements must be posted to inform all personnel, including the public, that entry into these areas subjects them to the security requirements. The posting should list the security conditions (see 41 CFR Part 102-74 Subpart C).

3. <u>PROPERTY PROTECTION AREAS (PPAs)</u>. PPAs are security areas that are established to protect employees and Government buildings, facilities and property.

   a. <u>General Requirements.</u> The requirements for PPAs must be configured to protect Government-owned property and equipment against damage, destruction, or theft and must provide a means to control public access. Protection may include physical barriers, access control systems, biometric systems, protective personnel or persons assigned administrative or other authorized security duties, intrusion detection systems, locks and keys, etc. The cognizant security authority must designate, describe, and document PPA protection measures within their SSP.

   b. <u>Signs</u>. Signs prohibiting <u>Trespassing</u>, Warning signs and/or notices must be posted around the perimeter and at entrances to a PPA. (see Chapter III). For General Services Administration (GSA) leased buildings and offices, GSA guidance implementing 41 CFR Part 102-74.365 describes the posting requirements.

      (1) Signs listing prohibited articles must be posted at PPA entrances. Additional prohibited and controlled article signs may be posted at inner security areas [Limited Area (LA), Exclusion Area (EA), Protected Area (PA) and/or Material Access Area (MAA)] as determined by the cognizant security authority. The listing of controlled articles is to be prepared by the sites.

(2) Warning signs and/or notices must be posted at entrances to areas under electronic surveillance advising that physical protection surveillance equipment is in operation.

c. Access Control. Access controls must be implemented to protect employees, property, and facilities. Security requirements for personnel and vehicles entering the PPA must be established by the cognizant security authority. Procedures for the processing of visitors, including foreign nationals must be approved by the cognizant security authority and documented in the SSP (see Attachment 2, DOE M 470.4-2A).

d. Parking Areas. If parking areas are near security areas and could interfere with intrusion detection sensor fields, clear zones, protective force (PF) operations, or pose a threat to target areas, these parking issues must be addressed in the SSP.

(1) Parking areas must not impact security equipment, security operations or be located in manner that degrades protection of Departmental interests.

(2) Vehicle bomb threats must be considered in determining the location of vehicle parking areas. For all new construction, parking areas should be located at a pre-determined distance from buildings to minimize a vehicle bomb threat. The set-back distance must be determined by using the site GSP and vulnerability assessment.

e. Inspection Program. An inspection program is to deter prohibited and controlled articles being brought into PPA facilities. All personnel, vehicles, packages, and hand-carried articles are subject to inspection before entry into a security area. Likewise, such programs must ensure that S&S interests are not removed. If implemented, the inspection program must be established by the cognizant security authority and documented in the SSP.

f. Intrusion Detection. If used, security requirements for intrusion detection, including long range detection technologies, for the PPA must be established by the cognizant security authority.

g. Visitor Processing. Site specific requirements and procedures for receiving visitors must be developed and approved by the cognizant security authority. For Exclusion Areas, Protected Areas, and Material Access Areas the procedures must provide for recording the following visitor information for paper entries: printed full name, and signature; organization represented; citizenship; person to be visited; purpose of visit; escort name; time of entry and exit. For electronic log entries; when using automatic access control systems; full name; agency or organization represented; citizenship; purpose of the visit; clearance level, if validated; escorts name and time of entry.

(1) Information from visitor logs must be retained in accordance with local records management procedures.

(2)   Paper visitor logs must plainly reflect the penalty of false personation and representation. Sites using electronic visitor processing must post signs reflecting the penalty for false personation and representation.

(a)   Laws regarding the penalty for false personating are stated in 18 U.S.C. Part 1, Section 911.

(b)   Laws regarding fraud and false statements are stated in 18 U.S.C., Part 1, Section 1001.

4.   LIMITED AREAS (LAs). LAs are security areas designated for the protection of classified matter and Category III and higher quantities of special nuclear material (SNM) and to serve as a concentric layer of protection. Specific protection requirements applicable to Category III quantities of SNM are provided in Appendix A.

a.   General Requirements. LA boundaries are defined by physical barriers encompassing the designated space and access controls to ensure that only authorized personnel are allowed to enter the LA.

b.   Signs. Signs must be posted to convey information on the prohibited and controlled articles; the inspection of vehicles, packages, hand-carried items, and persons entering or exiting the security area; the use of video surveillance equipment; and trespassing (see Title 42 United States Code (U.S.C.) Section 2278a). The decision on the signage and posting rests with the cognizant security authority and the requirements cited in federal statutes and regulations (see Chapter III).

c.   Access Control. The identity and clearance level of each person seeking entry to an LA must be validated by PF, or other appropriately authorized personnel, or by an automated system and documented in the SSP.

(1)   If automated access control equipment is used, a DOE security badge must be used to access the LA.

(2)   Entry control points for vehicle and pedestrian access to LAs must provide the same level of protection as that provided at all other points along the security perimeter.

(3)   Exits from LAs must satisfy life safety requirements of National Fire Protection Association (NFPA) 101, *Safety to Life from Fire in Buildings and Structures.* Some exits may be provided for emergency use only.

(a)   Security area entrances and exits must be equipped with doors, gates, rails, or other movable barriers that direct and control the movement of personnel or vehicles through designated control points.

    (b)   Automated gates must be designed to allow manual operation during power outages or mechanism failures.

    (c)   Site-specific requirements and procedures for receiving visitors must be developed and approved by the cognizant security authority. For Exclusion Areas, Protected Areas, and Material Access Areas, the procedures must provide for recording the following visitor information, for paper entries: printed full name and signature; organization represented; citizenship; person to be visited; purpose of visit; escort name; time of entry and exit. For electronic log entries; when using automatic access control systems; full name; agency or organization represented; citizenship; purpose of visit; clearance level, if validated; escorts name; and time of entry.

    (d)   Information from visitor logs must be retained in accordance with local records management procedures.

d.   <u>Personnel Access</u>. Individuals without a security clearance must be escorted by an authorized person who is to ensure measures are taken to prevent a compromise of classified matter.

    (1)   Escort Ratios. The cognizant security authority must establish escort-to-visitor ratios in a graded manner for each LA or above security area.

    (2)   Escort Responsibilities. Any person permitted to enter a LA or above who does not possess a security clearance at the appropriate level must be escorted at all times by an appropriately cleared and knowledgeable individual trained in local escort procedures.

        (a)   Escorts must ensure measures are taken to prevent compromise of S&S interests.

        (b)   The escort must ensure the visitor has a need-to-know for the security area or the S&S interests.

    (3)   Access Validation. Validations must occur at entry control points of LAs.

        (a)   The identity and security clearance held by each person seeking entry must be validated by appropriately authorized personnel, automated systems, or other means documented in the SSP.

        (b)   Where practicable, PF personnel will not be used to control access to LAs.

    (4)   "Piggybacking." The following requirements must be documented in the SSP if piggybacking into LAs is permitted.

(a)   Personnel with the appropriate security clearance may vouch for another person with the required security clearance to "piggyback" into an LA.

(b)   Authorized personnel permitting the entry of another person must inspect the individual's DOE security badge to ensure that it bears a likeness of the individual and that he or she has the proper security clearance identifier on the badge. When PF personnel are not controlling access to the LA, the DOE federal or contractor employee authorized to enter the LA is responsible for ensuring that those accompanying individuals are authorized entry.

(5)   Automated Access Control Systems. Automated access control systems may be used if the following requirements are met.

(a)   Automated access controls used for access to a LA or above security area must verify that DOE security badge is valid (i.e., that the badge data read by the system match the data assigned to the badge holder).

(b)   When remote, unattended, automated access control system entry control points are used for access to LA and above security areas, the barrier must be resistant to bypass. The unattended entry control point should have closed-circuit television system coverage.

(c)   Automated control system alarms (e.g., annunciation of a door alarm, duress alarm, tamper alarm, or anti-passback indication feature) must be treated as an intrusion alarm for the area being protected.

(d)   Personnel or other protective measures are required to protect card reader access transactions, displays (e.g., badge-encoded data), and keypad devices. The process of inputting, storing, displaying, or recording verification data must ensure that the data are protected in accordance with the SSP.

(e)   The system must record all attempts at access to include unsuccessful, unauthorized, and authorized.

(f)   Door locks opened by badge readers must be designed to relock immediately after the door has closed.

(g)   Transmission lines that carry security clearance and personal identification or verification data between devices/equipment must be protected in accordance with the SSP.

(h)   Records reflecting active assignments of DOE security badges, security clearance, and similar system-related records must be maintained. Records of personnel removed from the system must be retained for 1 year, unless a longer period is specified by other requirements. Personal data must be protected in conformance with the Privacy Act, (see 5 U.S.C. 552a).

(i)   Badge reader boxes, control lines, and junction boxes must have line supervision or tamper indication or be equipped with tamper-resistant devices. Data Gathering Panels/Field processors or multiplexers and other similar equipment must be tamper-alarmed or secured by a means that precludes surreptitious tampering with the equipment.

(j)   Uninterrupted power supply or compensatory measures must be provided at installations where continuous operation is required.

e.   Vehicle Access.

(1)   Approval for non-Government vehicles, which includes privately owned, to access LAs must be documented in the SSP.

(2)   Government-owned or -leased vehicles may be admitted only when on official business and only when operated by properly cleared and authorized drivers.

(3)   The SSP must identify procedures for inspection of, and access by, service and delivery vehicles. Factors to be considered are vehicle identification, identification of owner/operator and provision for various technologies to include vehicle navigation systems, cell phones and back-up cameras

(4)   All personnel within a vehicle are required to produce DOE security badges when accessing an LA and comply with individual LA procedures.

(5)   When a remote automated access control system is used for vehicle access control, it must verify that the operator or the escort has a valid DOE security badge (e.g., the badge data read by the system must match the data assigned to the badge holder).

5.   EXCLUSION AREAS (EAs). EAs are security areas that are bordered by physical barriers with access control that are established to protect classified matter where an individual's mere presence may result in access to classified matter. In addition to requirements for an LA, the following apply to an EA.

a.   General Requirements. The boundaries of EAs must be encompassed by physical barriers and be located within the minimum of an LA or receive approval of the cognizant security authority for those EAs not within a minimum of a LA.

b.   Access Control. In addition to the requirements for an LA the following requirements apply to access to an EA.

     (1)   Individuals permitted unescorted access must have the appropriate access authorizations and a need-to-know consistent with the classified matter to which they have access by virtue of their presence in the EA.

     (2)   Individuals without the appropriate security clearance and need-to-know must be escorted by a knowledgeable individual who must ensure measures are taken to prevent compromise of classified matter.

     (3)   Visitor logs must be used for EAs.

c.   Intrusion Detection.

     (1)   Unauthorized entry into the EA must be detected.

     (2)   When the exclusion area is unoccupied, and classified matter is not secured in a security container, then the EA must at a minimum, meet the requirements of a vault-type room (VTR) or an appropriate level of protection as determined by the cognizant security authority.

6.   SPECIAL DESIGNATED SECURITY AREAS. Other areas with access restrictions include CASs, secondary alarm stations (SASs), Sensitive Compartmented Information Facilities (SCIFs), Special Access Program Facilities (SAPFs), classified conferencing rooms, secure communications centers, and automated information system centers.

a.   Special Access Programs (SAP). The technical requirements for SAPs are identified in DOE M 471.2-3B, *Special Access Program Policies, Responsibilities, and Procedures*, dated 10-29-07, and DOE M 470.4-1.

b.   Alarm Stations. Security system requirements are described in Appendix B.

c.   Sensitive Compartmented Information Facilities. DOE follows the requirements in Director of Central Intelligence Directive (DCID) 6/9 and DCID Manual 6/9 dated 11-18-02, DOE O 5639.8A, *Security of Foreign Intelligence Information and Sensitive Compartmented Information Facilities*, dated 7-23-93, and DOE *Sensitive Compartmented Information Facility Procedural Guide* for the construction and accreditation of SCIFs.

d.   Other Designated Security Alarm Stations. If response to an alarm activity by LLEA/security personnel is permitted, then the alarm company/service must meet the specifications contained in Underwriters Laboratories (UL) Standard 827, *Standard for Central-Station Alarm Services*.

e.   Classified Conferencing Areas, Secure Communications Centers and Automated Information System Centers. (For the purpose of this section of the CRD the words "areas", "centers" and "facilities are terms for the location where the specified activity takes place).

(1) Classified information is to be protected in conformance with DOE Information Security policy (see DOE M 470.4-4A).

(2) Separate access controls and barriers must be established to restrict access to only persons employed in security communication and automated information centers handling classified information or otherwise requiring access to perform their official duties.

(3) Security clearances consistent with the highest level and category of classified information handled are required for all persons assigned to or having unescorted access to the above centers. A list of persons who have authorized access must be maintained within the center, and a record must be maintained of all visitors entering the facility.

(4) The design of automated information system centers and remote interrogation points that process classified information must consider the following:

(a) Establishment of a control zone consisting of the area above, below, and around equipment and distribution systems that have been inspected and are to be kept under physical and technical control to prevent unauthorized access, is required.

(b) Separate access controls and barriers. When contained within a larger designated security area, automated information system centers and remote interrogation points used to process classified information must have separate access controls and barriers.

(5) The selection of conferencing facilities for the conduct of classified meetings, and teleconferencing must conform to the provisions of DOE M 470.4-4A.

7. PROHIBITED AND CONTROLLED ARTICLES. Authorization for prohibited articles to be used for official Government business must be documented in a SSP. The articles listed below will not be permitted onto DOE property without appropriate authorization.

a. Prohibited Articles. Prohibited articles include items such as:

(1) explosives,

(2) dangerous weapons,

(3) instruments or material likely to produce substantial injury to persons or damage to persons or property,

(4)   controlled substances (e.g., illegal drugs and associated paraphernalia but not prescription medicine), and

(5)   other items prohibited by law. Specific information covering prohibited items may be found under the provisions of 10 CFR Part 860 and 41 CFR Part 102-74 Subpart C.

b.   Controlled Articles.

(1)   Controlled articles such as portable electronic devices, both Government and personally owned, capable of recording information or transmitting data (e.g., audio, video, radio frequency, infrared, and/or data link electronic equipment) are not permitted in limited areas (LAs), exclusion areas (EAs) protected areas (PAs), and material access areas (MAAs), without prior approval. The approval process must be documented in the SSP. NOTE: Government-owned computer systems which are part of the day-to-day operations are exempt from the requirement. The cognizant security authority must specify the equipment to be exempted from the approval process.

(2)   Sites are to develop procedures to account for, control, and limit all controlled articles entering specified security areas. These procedures must be approved by the cognizant security authority.

(a)   For application to Special Access Program Facilities (SAPFs), Sensitive Compartmented Information Facilities (SCIFs), etc., the Director Central Intelligence Directive (DCID) 6/9 and DCID manual, *Physical Security Standards for Sensitive Compartmented Information Facilities*, program guidance must be implemented. For SAPFs, the Programmatic policy addressing Controlled Articles, would be issued by the Special Access Program Administrator. (see DOE M 471.2-3B, *Special Access Program Polices, Responsibilities, and Procedures*).

(b)   Office of Secure Transportation Federal Agents, DOE protective personnel, and other Federal agents and Local Law Enforcement Officials with jurisdiction, whose duties routinely require the carrying and operation of controlled articles, are exempt from this requirement unless a nuclear safety reason exists to prohibit certain communication devices, e.g., cellular telephones, transceiver-radios and other electronic radiating/emitting devices. If such a prohibition exists, it is to be documented in specific agreements between the site and Federal and/or Local Law Enforcement agency.

CHAPTER III. POSTING NOTICES

1. <u>GENERAL REQUIREMENTS</u>. Signs must be posted at facilities, installations, and real property based on the need to implement Federal statutes protecting against degradation of S&S interests.

2. <u>TRESPASSING</u>. DOE property must be posted according to statutes, regulations, and the administrative requirements for posting specified in this CRD.

   a. <u>Statutory and Regulatory Provisions</u>.

      (1) Section 229 of the Atomic Energy Act of 1954 (42 U.S.C. 2278a) as implemented by 10 CFR 860, prohibits unauthorized entry and unauthorized carrying, transporting, or otherwise introducing or causing to be introduced any dangerous weapon, explosives, or other dangerous instrument or matter likely to produce substantial injury to persons or damage to property into or upon any facility, installation, or real property subject to the jurisdiction, administration, or in the custody of DOE. The statute provides for posting the regulations and penalties for violations.

      (2) Section 662 of the DOE Organization Act (42 U.S.C. 7270b), as implemented by 10 CFR 1048, prohibits unauthorized entry upon and unauthorized carrying, transporting, or otherwise introducing or causing to be introduced, any dangerous instrument or material likely to produce substantial injury to persons or damage to property into or onto the Strategic Petroleum Reserve, its storage or related facilities, or real property subject to the jurisdiction, administration, or custody of DOE. The statute provides for posting the regulations and penalties for violations.

      (3) Public Law 566, 80th Congress of June 1, 1948 (Title 40, U.S. Code 318); and the Federal Property and Administrative Services Act of 1949 (title 63, United States Statutes at Large, 377 as amended) provide the rules and regulations governing public buildings and grounds under the charge and control of the GSA. 41 CFR 102-74.365 Subpart C governs entry to public buildings and grounds under the charge and control of the GSA.

      (4) Signs prohibiting trespassing must be posted around the perimeter and at each entrance to a security area except when one security area is within a larger, posted security area. The distance between signage is to be determined by the cognizant security authority.

   b. <u>Posting Proposals</u>. Requirements for the administration of posting proposals are as follows:

(1) Conditions. Proposals for the posting of facilities, installations, or real property, or amendment to or revocation of a previous proposal must be submitted when one of the following occurs.

   (a) The property is owned by or contracted to the United States for DOE use.

   (b) The property requires protection under the Atomic Energy Act of 1954 and/or of the DOE Organization Act.

   (c) A previous notice needs to be amended or revoked.

(2) Contents.

   (a) Each posting proposal must include the name and specific location of the installation, facility, or real property to be covered and the boundary coordinates. If boundary coordinates are not available, the proposal must include a description that will furnish reasonable notice of the area to be covered, which may be an entire area or any portion thereof that can be physically delineated by the posting indicated in paragraph 2c below.

   (b) Each proposal for amendment or revocation must identify the property involved, state clearly the action to be taken (i.e., change in property description, correction, or revocation), and contain a new or revised property description, if required.

(3) Posting Requirements.

(4) Upon approval by the Office of Health, Safety and Security, with concurrence by the Office of General Counsel, a notice designating the facility, installation, or real property subject to the jurisdiction, administration, or in the custody of DOE must be published in the *Federal Register*. The notice is effective upon publication, providing the notices stating the pertinent prohibitions and penalties are posted (see 10 CFR 860.7).

(5) Property approved by the Office of Health, Safety and Security must be posted at entrances and at such intervals along the perimeter of the property to ensure notification of persons about to enter. Signs must measure at least 11 by 14 inches (28 x 36 centimeters).

(6) The signs should be configured with a white or yellow background and black lettering. Signs that notify of the use of deadly force should use a white background with red lettering for the words "WARNING USE OF DEADLY FORCE AUTHORIZED." The remaining words should be in black.

(7)   Placement of signs on fences must not interfere with the function of fence-mounted intrusion detection systems (IDS). If the signage interferes with the IDS or closed-circuit television coverage, it could be mounted on posts outside the fenced area. NOTE: The signage should be mounted midway between fence posts.

c.   Notification to the Federal Bureau of Investigation. Notification, by the program office exercising jurisdiction over the site/facility, of the date of posting, relocation, removal of posting, or other change, and the identity of the property involved must be furnished to the applicable office of the Federal Bureau of Investigation exercising investigative responsibility over the property.

CHAPTER IV. LOCKS AND KEYS

1. <u>GENERAL REQUIREMENTS</u>. A program to protect and manage locks and keys must be established by the cognizant security authority. The lock and key program must be applied in a graded manner based on the S&S interests being protected, identified threat, existing barriers, and other protection measures afforded these interests. Security keys include mechanical keys, key cards, and access codes. Security keys do not include administrative or privacy lock keys to factory-installed file cabinet locks, desk locks, toolboxes, etc. When access codes are used the codes must be protected from compromise.

2. <u>CATEGORIES</u>. Security keys and locks are divided into four levels, Levels I through IV. These levels are based on the S&S interest being protected and upon a site analysis. Non-security locks and keys are considered Administrative. The cognizant security authority must determine the appropriate level for application to the site. Facilities that do not possess nuclear weapons, weapons components, SNM, classified matter, and high-value government property should follow the requirements established for Level III and Level IV locks and keys.

    a. Level I. Security locations such as vaults, vault-type rooms, material access areas which store nuclear weapons and Category I and Category II that roll-up to a Category I quantity of SNM, and sensitive compartmented information facilities where Top Secret and/or Secret documents are stored require Level I security locks and keys.

    b. Level II. Building doors, entry control points, gates in PAs, fences, doors or other barriers or containers protecting Category II and Category III SNM and Confidential classified matter must be protected by locks and keys categorized as Level II.

    c. Level III. Buildings, gates in fences, cargo containers, and storage areas protecting Category IV SNM, and government property whose loss would adversely impact security and/or site/facility operations must be protected by locks and keys categorized as Level III.

    d. Level IV. Buildings where no classified matter or SNM is in use or stored should be protected by locks and keys categorized as Level IV.

    e. Administrative Keys. Desk, office, supply cabinets and vehicle keys are not considered security keys and have no control and accountability requirements based on the cognizant security authorities guidance. Keys to certain vehicle identified in the sites vulnerability analysis as a particular security concern will require added protection

3. <u>LOCK AND KEY STANDARDS</u>.

    a. Key locksets must meet American National Standards Institute (ANSI) Standard A156.2-1996, Grade 1, Bored and Preassembled Locks and Latches, or ANSI A156.13-1996, Grade 1, Mortise Locksets.

b. Locks used in the protection of classified matter and Categories I and II SNM (e.g., security containers, safes, vaults) must meet Federal Specification FF-L-2740A, Locks, Combination.

c. All security locks securing containers, vaults, and vault-type rooms placed into service after July 14, 1994 must have a lock that meets Federal Specification FF-L-2740A, Locks, Combination.

d. Combination padlocks must meet Federal Specification FF-P-110, Padlock, Changeable Combination, and standards cited in 41 CFR Part 101, Federal Property Management Regulations. These padlocks may be used with the lock bars securing metal filing cabinets.

e. Security key padlocks must meet the following specifications:

    (1) High-security, shrouded-shackle, key-operated padlocks must meet standards in Military Specification MIL-DTL-43607H, *Padlock, Key Operated, High Security, Shrouded Shackle*. High-security padlocks are approved to secure Category I and II SNM and Top Secret and/or Secret matter and are identified as a Level I.

    (2) Low-security, regular (open-shackle, key-operated padlocks) must meet the classes and standards in Commercial Item Description A-A-59486 and A-A-59487. The cognizant security authority must determine low-security padlock usage based upon the site analysis conducted on the security interest being protected.

    (3) Lock bars used to secure file cabinets containing classified information must be 1¼ inches (31.75 millimeters) by 3/16 inch (4.76 millimeters) or equivalent in cross section and constructed of rigid metal material. NOTE: Securing file cabinets with locking bars will not be acceptable after October 1, 2012.

    (4) Hasps and yokes on containers storing classified matter must be constructed of steel material, be at least ¼ inch (6.35 millimeters) in diameter or equivalent cross section, and be secured to the container by welding, or riveting, to preclude removal.

    (5) General field service padlock is a heavy-duty, exposed shackle lock that meets Federal Specification FF-P-2827. The key-operated padlock is designed for exposure to grit and corrosive or freezing environments. The cognizant security authority must determine general field service padlock usage based on a site analysis conducted on the security interest being protected.

f.   Panic hardware or emergency exit mechanisms used on emergency doors located in security areas must be operable only from inside the perimeter and must meet all applicable Life Safety Codes (see DOE M 470.4-7).

g.   Keys, key blanks, and key cutting codes must be protected in a graded fashion. Consideration must be given to the S&S interest being protected, the identified threat, existing barriers, and other protection measures afforded to the interest. Locks and keys must be categorized according to the interest being protected. An inventory and accountability system must be implemented.

h.   Security key stock must be stored in a manner to prevent loss, theft, or unauthorized use. (Security keys are devices that can open a lock and can include mechanical keys, key cards, access codes, and potentially other non-standard types of devices. Security keys do not include administrative or privacy lock keys to factory installed file cabinet locks, desk locks, toolboxes, etc.). Access codes that may open a lock that controls access to a security interest must be protected from compromise. Personnel responsible for the control and issuance of locking systems and/or security keys, including key cards (when used in place of mechanical keys), must maintain a security clearance commensurate with that required for access to the interest to which the keys provide direct access.

(1)   The organization responsible for the pinning and cutting of Levels I, II, and III security locks and keys must report to the cognizant security authority.

(2)   The pinning and cutting of Levels I, II, and III security locks and keys must be done within an LA or have equivalent type protection measures.

(3)   The use and protection strategy for grand master, master, sub-master, and control keys, etc., must be considered, analyzed and documented in the SSP. Master keys will not be used in the protection of Category I SNM.

4.   INVENTORY. An inventory system must be implemented to ensure the accountability of Levels I, II, and III security locks, keys, key rings, key ways, and pinned cores and documented in the SSP. A hands-on inventory must be conducted for all keys and padlocks both in use and in storage, as specified below. NOTE: The requirements for inventorying of locks do not apply to the XO series of combination locks installed on security containers and vaults/vault-type-rooms. Each accountable key and key core, including key cards (when used in place of mechanical keys), must have an affixed unique and permanent identifying number.

a.   Fabrication, issuance, return, and destruction of Levels I, II, and III security locks and keys must be documented.

(1)   Duplicate and replacement keys must not have the same key number assigned as the key being replaced or duplicated.

(2)   Grand master security keys must be kept to an operational minimum and protected at the highest level of S&S interest being protected. NOTE: Grand master security keys include a system wherein a series of locks are keyed alike.

(3)   The inventory record must identify the specific duplicate and replacement keys. If replaced, the disposition of the key being replaced must be recorded.

(4)   Include in inventory records locks, keys in possession of key holders, issuance stock, and keys assigned to key rings/key cabinets. The inventory record should include the list of the locations of locks that each key will open.

(5)   Document each person issued a Level I security lock and key and the individual who issued the locks and key.

(6)   Document the locations of the locks and keys.

b.   There must be a 100 percent inventory of all Level I security locks and keys.

(1)   Support the 100 percent inventory of Level I security locks and keys that must be performed on a semi-annual basis by the responsible organization.

(2)   An annual inventory must be conducted of locks in storage and all keys in storage or use.

(3)   Provide support in inventorying of Level I security keys not assigned to an individual (e.g., key rings, key cabinets, and keys issued on a temporary basis) that must be performed daily. Accountability of tamper indicating key rings is sufficient when used.

c.   Key rings for Level I and II must have a unique identifying number placed on the ring.

d.   Support a 100 percent inventory of all Levels II and III locks and keys on an annual basis by the responsible organization.

e.   When a Level I security key is unaccounted for, immediate notification must be made to the cognizant security authority, compensatory measures must be immediately initiated, and an incident of security concern inquiry must be completed. If the key cannot be located within 24 hours, the affected lock must be changed.

f.   Level IV locks and keys have no inventory requirement.

g.   Sites must have documented procedures for key turn-in when personnel or programs are terminating or when an individual no longer has a need for the key.

5.   LEVEL I SECURITY KEYS AND LOCKS.

     a.   Nuclear weapons, weapons components, Category I quantities of SNM, Category II quantities if SNM that credibly roll-up to a Category I quantity, certain high-value government property, and Secret or higher classified matter must be protected by locks and keys categorized as Level I. Level I key blanks must be restricted/proprietary; specifically, the blank must be unique to the site (e.g., it does not use a commercially available master key blank).

     b.   Once they are put in service inside a PA, Level I security locks and keys must not leave the PA without authorization as described in the SSP. Any key that leaves the PA without authorization shall be considered unaccounted for and reported as lost. When not in use for the protection of the above interests (e.g., locksmith service work) the assembled Level I security locks or cores and Level I security keys must remain under the direct control of an authorized person or must be stored in a General Services Administration (GSA)-approved security container or a vault-type room (or other location as identified in the SSP with equivalent protection). Access to the Level I security locks and keys must be controlled and limited to authorized personnel.

     c.   Sites must conduct and document an assessment of duties for possible enrollment of locksmith personnel into the DOE Human Reliability Program (10 CFR 712).

     d.   Any installation, replacement, or maintenance activities associated with Level I security locks must be documented to include the name of a person who performed the activity.

     e.   The number of Level I keys must be kept to an operational minimum.

     f.   Level I keys must be on a separate key ring from all other levels of keys.

     g.   All parts of broken Level I security keys should be recovered. If the functional part of the key (the blade) is lost or not retrievable, it must be reported as a lost/missing key as required by Impact Measurement Index (IMI) categorization cited in Section N, DOE M 470.4-1.

     h.   Obsolete, damaged, or inoperative Level I keys must be destroyed in a manner authorized by the cognizant security authority and the destruction recorded.

     i.   In order for corrective actions to be taken quickly after an incident involving the loss, theft, or destruction of a Level I lock or key, a risk assessment and compensatory measures must be pre-established and documented.

6.   LEVEL II SECURITY KEYS AND LOCKS.

     a.   Level II security locks and keys must be used to control access to Category II and Category III SNM as well as Confidential classified matter. These typically are used for building doors, entry control points, gates in PA fences, LA doors or other barriers or containers. When not in use for the protection of the above interests (e.g., locksmith service work) the Assembled Level II security locks or cores and Level II security keys must remain under the direct control of an authorized person or must be stored in a GSA-approved security container or a vault-type room (or other location as identified in the SSP with equivalent protection). Access to the Level II security locks and keys must be controlled and limited to authorized personnel.

 b. The number of Level II keys must be kept to an operational minimum.

 c. Level II locks and keys once put into service must not leave the site without cognizant security authority approval.

 d. All parts of broken Level II security keys should be recovered; if the functional part of the key (the blade) is lost or not retrievable, it must be reported as a lost/missing key.

 e. Obsolete, damaged, or inoperative Level II keys must be destroyed in a manner authorized by the cognizant security authority and the destruction recorded.

 f. Incidents involving Level II keys and locks must be reported (see IMI categorization cited in DOE M 470.4-1).

7. <u>LEVEL III SECURITY KEYS AND LOCKS</u>.

 a. Level III security locks and keys control access to Category IV SNM and Government property and are typically associated with buildings, gates in fences, cargo containers, and storage areas.

 b. All parts of broken Level III security keys must be recovered; if the functional part of the key (the blade) is lost or not retrievable, it must be reported to the cognizant security authority.

 c. Obsolete, damaged, or inoperative Level III keys must be destroyed in a manner authorized by the cognizant security authority and such destruction recorded.

 d. Site-specific procedures must be developed for the control of Level III security locks and keys and be approved by the cognizant security authority.

 e. If a Level III lock or key is discovered to be missing or tampered with, the incident must be reported to DOE Headquarters (see DOE M 470.4-1), unless the cognizant security authority re-evaluates the IMI categorization level.

8. <u>LEVEL IV SECURITY KEYS AND LOCKS</u>. Level IV locks and keys are typically used for buildings or offices where there is no open storage of classified matter and no classified matter in use. Desk, office and vehicle keys are considered administrative and have no control and accountability requirements.

CHAPTER V. MAINTENANCE

1. GENERAL REQUIREMENTS. Security-related subsystems and components must be maintained in operable condition. A regularly scheduled testing and maintenance program must be established and documented.

2. CORRECTIVE MAINTENANCE. Corrective maintenance must be performed on site-determined critical and non-critical system elements.

    a. Compensatory Measures. Compensatory measures must be implemented immediately when any part of a critical system element protecting vital equipment, Top Secret matter, SCI or SAP interests is out of service. Compensatory measures must be continued until maintenance is complete and the system element is back in service.

    b. Corrective Maintenance within 24 Hours. Corrective maintenance must be initiated within 24 hours of receiving a report that there has been a malfunction of a site-determined critical system element protecting vital equipment, Top Secret matter, SCI or SAP interests.

    c. Corrective Maintenance within 72 Hours. Corrective maintenance must be initiated within 72 hours of detection of a malfunction for all other system elements protecting, vital equipment, Top Secret matter SCI or SAP interest.

    d. Other Corrective Maintenance. Corrective maintenance procedures for systems protecting Secret or Confidential matter must be approved by the cognizant security authority and prescribed in site operation procedures.

    e. Non-Critical System Maintenance. For non-critical system elements, the cognizant security authority must approve compensatory measure implementation procedures.

3. PREVENTIVE MAINTENANCE. Preventive maintenance must be performed on S&S-related subsystems and components in accordance with manufacturers' specifications and/or local procedures. Remote maintenance of active systems shall not be performed by uncleared personnel.

4. MAINTENANCE PERSONNEL SECURITY CLEARANCES. Personnel who test, maintain, or service critical system elements must have security clearances consistent with the S&S interest being protected. The cognizant security authority may approve local procedures to allow uncleared system maintenance/repair personnel to perform required service providing system integrity cannot be compromised and the system and/or component integrity verified.

    a. Security clearances are not required when testing and maintenance are performed as bench services away from the security area.

b.   Systems or critical system elements bench-tested or maintained away from the security area by personnel without the appropriate security clearances must be inspected and operationally tested by qualified and cleared personnel before being returned to service.

c.   Personnel who test, maintain, or service non-critical system elements must have security clearances consistent with the S&S interest being protected as determined by the cognizant security authority.

5.   <u>TESTING AND MAINTENANCE OF SCREENING EQUIPMENT</u>. Screening equipment can include explosive detectors, metal detectors, and x-ray systems and must be capable of detecting prohibited and controlled articles are detected before being permitted into Department of Energy facilities.

a.   The following should be used as standard test weapons for metal detectors or the site must implement the performance testing procedures and test objects cited in Sections 5.1, 5.2 and the portion of 5.3 of NIJ Standard 0601.02, Law Enforcement and Corrections Standards and Testing Program, relating to non-ferromagnetic stainless steel knives:

(1)   steel and aluminum alloy .25 caliber automatic pistol manufactured in Italy by Armi Tanfoglio Giuseppe, sold in the United States by Excam as Model GT27B and by F.I.E. as the Titan (weight: about 343 grams); or

(2)   aluminum, model 7, .380 caliber Derringer manufactured by American Derringer Corporation (weight: about 200 grams); and

(3)   stainless steel 0.22 caliber long rifle mini-revolver, manufactured by North American Arms (weight: about 129 grams).

b.   X-ray machines may be used to supplement metal detectors and protective personnel hand searches for prohibited and controlled articles.

(1)   X-ray machines must provide a discernable image of prohibited and controlled articles.

(2)   X-ray machines must image an unobstructed (discernable) set of wires (ASTM) standard for test objects (see ASTM Standard F792-01e2, *Standard Practice for Evaluating the Imaging Performance of Security X-ray Systems*).

6.   <u>RECORD KEEPING</u>.

a.   Record of the failure and repair of all communication equipment must be maintained so that type of failure, unit serial number, and equipment type can be compiled.

    b.   Testing and maintenance records must be retained in accordance with the requirements of approved records management procedures.

CHAPTER VI. BARRIERS

1. GENERAL REQUIREMENTS. Physical barriers serve as the physical demarcation of the security area. Barriers such as fences, walls, and doors or activated barriers must be used to deter and delay unauthorized access. At a minimum, an analysis is required of high consequence security areas to determine the protection measures against Vehicle Borne Improvised Explosive Devices (VBIED). Barriers may be used to support the prevention of stand-off-attacks.

    a. Barriers must be used to direct the flow of personnel and vehicular traffic through designated entry control points to permit efficient operation of access controls and entry point inspections and to provide the ability to identify and engage adversaries along all feasible pathways.

    b. Entry control points must be designed to provide a barrier resistant to bypass.

    c. Permanent barriers must be used to enclose security areas, except during construction or temporary activities, when temporary barriers may be erected.

    d. Barriers such as fences, walls, and doors may be used to identify the boundary of the property protection area and to provide protection. Barriers must be capable of controlling, impeding, or denying access to a security area.

    e. Fences used should be installed no closer than 20 feet (6 meters) from the building or S&S interest being protected.

2. PENETRATION OF SECURITY AREA BARRIERS. Penetration of security area barrier requirements include the following.

    a. Elevators that penetrate a security area barrier must be provided with an access control system that is equivalent to the access control requirements for the security area being penetrated.

    b. Utility corridors that penetrate security area barriers must provide the same degree of penetration resistance as the barriers they penetrate.

    c. Objects that intruders could use to scale or bridge barriers and enter security areas must be removed or secured to prevent their unauthorized use.

    d. If a security area configuration is altered, barriers must be erected (e.g., during construction or temporary activities), and at a minimum, a risk assessment must be conducted to validate equivalent protection measures.

    e. The barrier design must consider proximity to buildings or overhanging structures.

3. HARDWARE. Screws, nuts, bolts, hasps, clamps, bars, wire mesh, hinges, and hinge pins must be fastened securely to preclude removal and to ensure visual evidence of tampering. Hardware accessible from outside the security area must be peened, brazed, or spot-welded to preclude removal or the area must be otherwise secured by use of tamper-resistant hardware (e.g., non-removable hinge pins) or by other means as described in the SSP. NOTE: These requirements do not apply to fencing.

4. FENCING. When used to protect security areas designated as LAs or higher, fencing must meet the following requirements.

    a. Fencing Materials and Specifications.

        (1) Chain link fabric consisting of a minimum of No. 11 American Wire Gauge (AWG) or heavier galvanized steel wire with mesh openings not larger than 2 inches (5.08 centimeters) on a side must be used at security areas. This fencing must be topped by three or more strands of barbed wire mounted on single or double outriggers. Double outriggers may be topped with coiled barbed wire (or with a barbed tape coil). The direction of the outrigger is at the discretion of the cognizant security authority.

        (2) Overall fence height, excluding barbed wire or barbed tape coil topping, must be a minimum of 7 feet (2.13 meters).

        (3) Fence lines must be kept clear of vegetation, trash, equipment, and other objects that could impede observation or facilitate bridging.

        (4) Gate hardware that if removed would facilitate unauthorized entry must be installed in a manner to mitigate tampering and/or removal (e.g., by brazing, peening, or welding).

        (5) Posts, bracing, and other structural members must be located on the inside of security fences.

        (6) Wire ties used to fasten fence fabric to poles must be of equal tensile strength to that of the fence fabric.

    b. Permanent Security Fencing. When permanent fencing is used to enclose LAs or higher, fencing must meet the following construction requirements.

        (1) Areas under security fencing subject to water flow, such as bridges, culverts, ditches, and swales, must be blocked with wire or steel bars that provide for the passage of floodwater but also provide a penetration delay equal to that of the security fence.

        (2) Depressions where water flow is not a problem must be covered by additional fencing suspended from the lower rail of the main fencing.

(3) Fencing must extend to within 2 inches (5.08 centimeters) of firm ground or below the surface if the soil is unstable or subject to erosion.

(a) Surfaces must be stabilized in areas where loose sand, shifting soils, or surface waters may cause erosion and thereby assist an intruder in penetrating the area.

(b) Where surface stabilization is impossible or impractical, concrete curbs, sills, or a similar type of anchoring device extending below ground level must be provided.

(4) Alternate barriers may be used if the penetration resistance of the barrier is equal to or greater than security fencing specified in this chapter.

c. Temporary Security Fencing. Temporary barriers may be of any height and material that effectively impedes access to the area. During construction or temporary activities, security fencing must be installed to:

(1) exclude unauthorized vehicular and pedestrian traffic from the security area site,

(2) restrict authorized vehicular traffic to designated access roads, and

(3) comply with site-specific protection goals and operational requirements.

5. PERIMETER BARRIER GATES. Controls for motorized gates used for entry control points must be located within protective force posts or other locations as described in the SSP. Motorized gates must be designed to facilitate manual operation during power outages.

6. EXTERIOR WALLS. Walls that constitute exterior barriers of security areas must extend from the floor to the structural ceiling unless equivalent means are used to provide evidence of penetration of the security area or access to the security interest being protected.

7. CEILING AND FLOORS. Ceilings and floors must be constructed of building materials that offer penetration resistance to, and evidence of, unauthorized entry into the area.

8. DOORS. Doors, door frames, and door jambs associated with walls serving as barriers must provide the necessary barrier delay required by the SSP. Requirements include the following.

a. Penetration Resistance Doors. Doors with transparent glazing material must offer penetration resistance to, and evidence of, unauthorized entry into the area. Doors that serve exclusively as emergency and evacuation exits from security areas must:

(1) not be accessible from outside the security area,

(2)   comply with NFPA 101, and

(3)   not open into spaces of greater security.

b.   Astragals or Mullions. An astragal or mullion must be used where doors used in pairs meet. Door louvers, baffles, or astragals/mullions must be reinforced and immovable from outside the area being protected.

c.   Visual Access. A sight baffle must be used if visual access is a factor.

9.   WINDOWS. The following design requirements must be applied to security windows when used as physical barriers.

a.   Windows must offer penetration resistance to, and evidence of, unauthorized entry into the area.

b.   Frames must be securely anchored in the walls and windows locked from the inside or installed in fixed (non-operable) frames so the panes are not removable from outside the area under protection.

c.   Visual barriers must be used if visual access is a factor.

10.   MISCELLANEOUS OPENINGS. The following requirements apply to security areas other than GAAs and PPAs. The application to GAAs and PPAs is at the discretion of the cognizant security authority based on a risk assessment.

a.   Utility and Other Barrier Penetrations and Openings. Physical protection features must be implemented at all locations where miscellaneous openings occur, such as where storm sewers, drainage swales, and site utilities intersect the security boundary or area. Miscellaneous openings/penetrations must be sealed/filled or constricted barriers applied to deter and/or prevent a determined threat. In those instances where a potential audio/video surveillance threat could occur within conference rooms and other similar facilities approved for classified discussions the provisions of DOE M 470.4-4A should be implemented.

b.   Criteria. Barriers or alarms are required for all miscellaneous openings for which:

(1)   the opening is larger than 96 square inches (619.20 square centimeters) in area and larger than 6 inches (15.24 centimeters) in the smallest dimension and/or the opening is located within 18 feet (5.48 meters) of the ground, roof, or ledge of a lower security area;

(2)   the opening is located within 14 feet (4.26 meters) diagonally or directly opposite a window, fire escape, roof, or other opening in an uncontrolled adjacent building;

(3)   the opening is not visible from another controlled opening in the same barrier; or

(4)   the opening is below a perimeter barrier, which is part of a utility tunnel, pipe chase, exhaust ducts or air handling filter banks penetrating the building, facility, or site.

CHAPTER VII. COMMUNICATIONS, ELECTRICAL POWER AND LIGHTING

1. <u>COMMUNICATIONS</u>. Communications equipment must be provided to facilitate reliable information exchanges between protective force personnel. Security system transmission lines and data must be protected in a graded manner from tampering and substitution.

    a. <u>Loss of Primary Power</u>. Systems must remain operable during the loss and recovery of primary electrical power.

    b. <u>Communication Systems</u>. Protection system communications must support two vital functions: alarm communication/display and protective force (PF) communications. PF communications include the procedures and hardware that enable officers to communicate with each other.

2. <u>ELECTRICAL POWER</u>. Power supply elements located or operating within the confines of the site should be protected from malicious physical attacks based on a documented local site determination of impact. The site must determine the need for auxiliary power based on other safeguards and security interests being protected and document it in the SSP.

3. <u>LIGHTING</u>. Lighting systems must allow for detection and assessment of unauthorized persons. Protective system lighting must:

    a. enable assessment of unauthorized activities and/or persons at pedestrian and vehicular entrances and allow examination of DOE security badges and inspections of personnel, hand-carried items, packages, and vehicles;

    b. be positioned so that PF personnel are not spotlighted, blinded, or silhouetted by the lights, and the lighting placement and design should enhance, not minimize, PF night-vision capabilities;

    c. ensure that compensatory measures identified in the SSP are implemented when the lighting system fails;

    d. be maintained and tested in accordance with locally approved procedures;

    e. not illuminate patrol paths or PF personnel manning fixed posts other than at entry control points;

    f. illuminate the area outside the fence line or barrier so that it will expose anyone approaching the coverage area and limit the vision of anyone outside of the fence or barrier;

    g. complement the electro-optical/closed-circuit television (CCTV) assessment systems;

     h.   illuminate the area within the fence/barrier boundary or the exterior of a building;

     i.   be configured so that an intruder cannot defeat the system by easily gaining access to the lighting controls and turning-off the system; and

     j.   allow for the rapid and reliable assessment of alarms from either the CCTV system or PF personnel.

CHAPTER VIII. SECURE STORAGE

1.   <u>GENERAL REQUIREMENTS</u>.

   a.   <u>Secure Storage</u>. The storage requirements for classified matter can be found in Information Security policy (see DOE M 470.4-4A).

   b.   <u>Access Controls</u>. Access to vaults and VTRs must be strictly controlled and based on an appropriate security clearance and need-to-know.

      (1)   Persons without need-to-know and the appropriate security clearance must be escorted at all times.

      (2)   Protective measures to mask classified matter must be used before visitors or cleared persons without need-to-know receive access.

      (3)   Means of controlling access must be documented in a SSP.

      (4)   Access controls at vaults and VTRs must provide logging or recording of all personnel entries and exits including visitors. Logged or recorded entries must include the identification/name and date/time of entry and exit of the individual and the escort as required.

         (a)   In vaults and VTRs where entering personnel are restricted from access (e.g., a foyer) to SNM or classified matter, logging entry and exit is not required.

         (b)   The cognizant security authority may waive the requirement for repeated logging for personnel whose offices are located within the boundary of the vaults and VTRs. Initial daily entry and final daily exit logging are required.

   c.   <u>Miscellaneous Openings</u>. Any miscellaneous openings of a size and shape to permit unauthorized entry [larger than 96 square inches (619.2 square centimeters) in area and more than 6 inches (15.24 centimeters) in its smallest dimension] must be equipped with barriers such as wire mesh, 9-gauge expanded metal, or rigid steel bars at least 0.5 inches (1.3 centimeters) in diameter secured in a way to prevent unauthorized removal e.g., welded vertically and horizontally 6 inches (15.24 centimeters) on center. The rigid steel bars must be securely fastened at both ends to preclude removal. Where used, wire mesh, expanded metal, or rigid steel bars must be mounted so that classified matter or SNM cannot be removed. When pipe or conduit pass through a wall, the annular space between the sleeve and the pipe or conduit must be filled to show evidence of surreptitious removal.

2.   <u>VAULTS AND VAULT-TYPE ROOMS</u>. The standards required for construction of vaults and vault-type rooms, other than GSA-approved modular vaults, apply to all new construction, reconstruction, alterations, modifications and repairs.

Vault construction standards must comply with Federal Standard 832, Construction Methods and Materials for Vaults.

Vault-type room construction standards must comply with the requirements of this Manual. The cognizant security authority must approve all construction types and the methods used before the storage of classified matter or S&S interests is authorized.

a.   Vaults. A vault must be a penetration-resistant, windowless enclosure that has doors, walls, floor, and roof/ceiling designed and constructed to significantly delay penetration from forced entry and equipped with intrusion detection system devices on openings allowing access. The material thickness must be determined by the requirement for forcible entry delay times for the safeguards and security interest stored within but must not be less than the delay time provided by a minimum 8-inch (20.32-centimeters)-thick reinforced concrete poured in place, with a minimum 28-day compressive strength of 2,500 pounds per square inch (17,237 kilopascal). Technologies such as activated barriers or passive/active denial systems may be used in lieu of thicker concrete when analysis indicates that delay times exceeding that of 8-inch (20.32-centimeters)-thick reinforced concrete are required. The site's analysis of protection measures used must be documented in its site security plan. For new vault construction, Federal Standard 832, *Federal Standard Construction Methods and Materials for Vaults* must be used.

(1)   Vault Door. A vault door and frame must meet the GSA's highest level of penetration resistance. The lock on the door must be a minimum of a GSA-approved lock.

(2)   Wall Penetrations. Any miscellaneous openings of a size and shape to permit unauthorized entry [larger than 96 square inches (619.2 square centimeters} in area and more than 6 inches (15.24 centimeters) in its smallest dimension] must be equipped with barriers such as wire mesh, 9-gauge expanded metal or rigid steel bars at least 0.5 inches (1.3 centimeters) in diameter secured in a way to prevent unauthorized removal; e.g., welded vertically and horizontally 6 inches (15.24 centimeters) on center. The rigid steel bars must be securely fastened at both ends to preclude removal. Where used, wire mesh, expanded metal, or rigid steel bars must be mounted so that special nuclear material (SNM) cannot be removed. The annular space between the sleeve and the pipe or conduit must be filled to show evidence of surreptitious removal.

(3)   Modular Vaults. A modular vault approved by the GSA may be used in lieu of a vault for the storage of classified matter. The modular vault must be equipped with a GSA-approved vault door with locks and intrusion detection alarms as specified in paragraph 4b of this chapter.

b.   Vault-Type Room. The perimeter walls, floors, and ceiling must be permanently constructed and attached to one another. All construction must be done in a manner that provides visual evidence of unauthorized penetration. The walls, floor, ceiling and door and door frame must be constructed of materials which provide comparable penetration resistance. The following standards are required for all new construction, reconstruction, alterations, modifications, and repairs of existing areas.

(1)   Hardware. Hardware must be fastened in such a way to reveal or preclude surreptitious removal and to ensure visual evidence of tampering. Hardware accessible from outside the area must be peened, pinned, brazed, or spot-welded to preclude removal.

(2)   Floors and Walls. Construction materials must offer resistance to and evidence of unauthorized entry into the VTR. If insert-type panels are used, a method must be devised to prevent their removal without leaving visual evidence of tampering.

(a)   Should any of the outer walls/floors or ceilings be adjacent to space not controlled by DOE, the walls must be constructed of or reinforced with more substantial building materials such as brick, concrete, corrugated metal, wire mesh, etc.

(b)   If visual access is a factor, barrier walls must be opaque or translucent.

(3)   Windows. Windows that can be routinely opened and are installed at a height of less than 18 feet (5.48 meters) from any point adjacent to the window that would permit unrestricted access must be provided with protective measures to delay or deter entry or to notify the response force of an attempted entry.

(a)   If visual access is a security concern, the windows must be closed and locked and must be translucent or opaque.

(b)   During non-working hours, the windows must be closed and securely fastened to preclude surreptitious entry.

(4)   Doors. Doors must be of wood or metal. Windows, door louvers, baffle plates or service panels, or similar openings must be secured on the inside with 18-gauge expanded metal or wire mesh to preclude unauthorized entry. Wooden doors must be of solid core construction, 1.75 inches (4.445 centimeters) thick, or faced on the exterior side with at least 16-gauge sheet metal.

(a)   If visual access is a security concern, the opening or window must be baffled or must be covered with translucent or opaque coverings.

(b)   When doors are used in pairs, an astragal must be installed where the doors meet.

(c)   When door louvers or baffle plates are used, they must be reinforced with 18-gauge expanded metal or wire mesh fastened inside the VTR. If visual access is a concern, openings must be baffled or must be covered with translucent or opaque coverings.

(5)   Ceilings.

(a)   When barrier walls do not extend to the true ceiling and a false ceiling is created, the false ceiling must be reinforced with 18-gauge expanded metal or wire mesh to serve as a true ceiling or ceiling tile clips must be secured. When barrier walls do extend to the true ceiling, reinforcements are not required.

<u>1</u>   Any wire mesh or expanded metal used must overlap the adjoining walls and be secured to show evidence of any tampering.

<u>2</u>   When ceiling tile clips are used, a minimum of four clips per tile must be installed. If the ceiling tile cannot accommodate four clips, the maximum number of clips that can be accommodated on the tile must be used. The clips must be installed from the interior of the area, and each clip must be mounted to preclude surreptitious entry.

(b)   In some instances, it may not be practical to erect a solid suspended ceiling as part of the VTR. For example, in VTRs where overhead cranes are used to move bulky equipment, the air-conditioning system may be impeded by the construction of a solid suspended ceiling, or the height of the security interest may make a suspended ceiling impractical. In such cases, special provisions such as motion detection systems must be used to ensure that the area cannot be entered surreptitiously by going over the top of the walls.

3.   <u>VAULT-TYPE ROOM (VTR) COMPLEX</u>. Vault-type room S&S criteria may be extended to multiple rooms including an entire building. VTR complexes must meet the standards and construction requirements identified in paragraph 2b(5) above.

a.   Interior walls may extend to a false ceiling and/or raised floor. Interior doors, windows, and openings may exist between different work areas. The requirement to detect unauthorized access may be accomplished through direct visual observation by an individual authorized in the area or through intrusion detection sensors.

b. Protective measures must ensure that the security interest is surrounded by an IDS or that the entire surrounding perimeter (walls, ceiling and floor) is able to detect penetration. For a building within a PA, a perimeter intrusion detection and assessment system that surrounds the entire building perimeter meets the IDS requirement. This does not preclude the requirement for an IDS within each VTR.

4. INTRUSION DETECTION SYSTEMS. IDSs are required for vaults and VTRs and in some instances where certain types of containers are used to store S&S interests. At vaults and VTRs containing Top Secret, SNM, or open storage of classified information, the IDS must be placed in secure mode when the vault or VTR is unoccupied. In all cases, the IDS must be placed in secure mode at the end of daily operations.

a. Vaults. Doors or openings allowing access into vaults must be equipped with IDS devices. A balanced magnetic switch (BMS) or other equally effective device must be used on each door or movable opening to allow detection of attempted or actual unauthorized access.

b. Vault-Type Rooms. In addition to the requirements listed below, a BMS or equivalent device must be used on each door or movable opening to allow detection of attempted or actual unauthorized access. At a VTR designated for the open storage of classified matter, protective measures must ensure that that the security interest is surrounded by an IDS or that the entire surrounding perimeter (walls, ceiling and floor) is able to detect penetration.

(1) IDS sensors are to be used to detect movement within the VTR envelope, sensor coverage must ensure that the security interest is surrounded by an IDS such that physical access is detected via any credible pathway. Where visual access is a concern, detection must occur prior to the point where visual access becomes possible.

(a) The cognizant security authority may require the installation of sensors in the false floor area (or ceiling) if the distance exceeds 6 inches (15.24 centimeters). If the requirements of this paragraph are not implemented, paragraph (b) must also be considered.

(b) The interests under protection must be considered when not requiring the installation of sensors between the true floor (or ceiling) and the false floor (or ceiling).

(2) Where IDS sensors are used to detect movement within a vault-type room, sensors must provide coverage of credible pathways from the exterior barrier to the matter being protected.

5. SECURITY CONTAINERS. The GSA establishes the national standards and specifications for commercially manufactured security containers or cabinets. Containers purchased after July 14, 1994, must conform to the latest GSA standards and specifications. Steel filing cabinets with rigid metal lock bar and approved three position, dial-type, changeable combination locks, purchased and approved for storage of SECRET material may continue to be used until October 1, 2012. If steel filing cabinets are used to store classified matter, the supplemental controls specified in DOE M 470.4-4A must be implemented.

    a. Requirements.

        (1) Label and Mark. A security container must bear a test certification label on the inside of the locking drawer or door and must be marked "GSA-Approved Security Container" on the outside of the top drawer or door.

        (2) Maintenance. A history for each security container describing damage sustained and repairs accomplished must be recorded on Optional Form 89, *Maintenance Record for Security Containers/Vault Doors* and retained for the life of the security container.

    b. Damage and Repair of GSA-Approved Security Containers. Neutralizing lock-outs or repairing any damage that affects the integrity of a security container approved for the storage of classified information must be conducted by cleared or escorted safe technicians or locksmiths.

        (1) Requirements in Federal Standard 809, *Neutralization and Repair of GSA Approved Containers*, must be met for neutralization and repair of GSA-approved containers and vault doors.

        (2) Physically modified containers are not approved by GSA.

6. NON-CONFORMING STORAGE. Non-Conforming Storage is a means of providing equivalent storage protection for classified matter that cannot be protected by established standards and requirements due to size, nature, operational necessity, or other factors. Authority and protection requirements for non-conforming storage are provided in DOE M 470.4-4A.

CHAPTER IX. INTRUSION DETECTION AND ASSESSMENT SYSTEMS

1. <u>GENERAL REQUIREMENTS</u>. The intrusion detection and assessment system is configured to support interior and exterior applications. Intrusion detection and assessment systems and/or visual observation by protective force personnel must be used to protect classified matter, Government property, and SNM to ensure breaches of security barriers or boundaries are detected and alarms annunciate. The systems must be configured so that only authorized personnel may make adjustments.

    a. Intrusion detection and assessment systems must function effectively in all environmental conditions and under all types of lighting conditions or compensatory measures must be implemented.

    b. An effective method must be established for assessing all IDS alarms (e.g., line supervision, intrusion, false, nuisance, system failure, tamper, and radio frequency alarms when radio frequency is used) to determine the cause.

    c. IDS alarms used for the protection of S&S interests must be assessed immediately by either the PF, central alarm station (CAS)/ secondary alarm station (SAS) personnel via closed-circuit television (CCTV), or by other authorized personnel as identified in the SSP.

    d. Response capability to IDS alarms must be provided to protect S&S interests.

    e. The response capability must be provided by assigned PF personnel, by local law enforcement agency, or other authorized personnel as documented in the SSP.

    f. Systems, system components, and critical system elements must be performance-tested at a documented frequency commensurate with the established requirements (see DOE M 470.4-1).

    g. The testing program for systems and system components must be developed and implemented in locally developed security planning documents.

    h. Performance testing must be conducted to validate system effectiveness.

    i. Performance testing should be conducted to determine the proper settings for high detection rates with the lowest possible nuisance alarm rates. Tests should be performed along credible pathways with a low-profile target (crawling) and a higher velocity and profile targets (walking, running, fast-crawl, rolling) or as appropriate given space considerations for interior applications. If assessment is by CCTV, the tests should be conducted under the lowest lighting conditions that are routinely available. The testing should be conducted against the worst case "light to dark ratio" to determine if shadows or dark spots in the field of view degrade assessment viability.

    j. Testing must ensure that the alarm communication line or data link is capable of transmitting an alarm signal and that it has not been compromised.

k.   The IDS must be designed, installed, operated, and maintained to ensure that the number of false and nuisance alarms do not reduce system effectiveness.

    (1)   The false and nuisance threshold rates are determined after analysis and evaluation. The cognizant security authority develops written False Alarm Rates (FAR)/Nuisance Alarm Rates (NAR) parameters based on the analysis and site specific conditions, seeking to achieve "As Low As Reasonably Achievable" (ALARA) levels. However, at a minimum:

        (a)   Each interior intrusion detection sensor should not have a false or nuisance alarm rate of more than one alarm per 2400 hours of operation while maintaining proper detection sensitivity.

        (b)   Each exterior intrusion detection sensor should not have a false or nuisance alarm rate of more than one alarm per 24 hours of operation while maintaining proper detection sensitivity.

        (c)   Interior IDS used to protect munitions/explosives storage igloos/bunkers should not have false or nuisance alarm rates exceeding one alarm per 400 hours of operation while maintaining proper detection sensitivity.

    (2)   If the alarms can be assessed at all times, either visually or by CCTV, a higher nuisance alarm rate may be tolerated if such alarms do not degrade system effectiveness. Although higher rates may be tolerated, each alarm occurrence, regardless of the cause, must be documented for analysis and trending purposes.

2.   <u>INTERIOR IDS REQUIREMENTS</u>. The following requirements apply to interior IDS:

a.   <u>Interior Systems</u>. Interior systems must be designed, installed, and maintained to deter adversaries from circumventing the detection system. Interior systems must be installed to eliminate gaps in detection coverage.

    (2)   The IDS must be tested when installed and annually (at least every 12 months) thereafter.

    (3)   If testing indicates degradation of the IDS, it must be repaired and retested.

    (4)   Interior IDSs may be used as compensatory measures for unattended entry/exit points, utility ducts, or other openings meeting the unattended openings requirements contained in this CRD.

b.   <u>Balanced Magnetic Switches</u>. BMSs must initiate an alarm upon attempted substitution of an external magnetic field when the switch is in the normal secured position and whenever the leading edge of the door is moved 1 inch (2.5 centimeters) from the door jamb.

c. Volumetric Devices. Tests for volumetric interior IDSs must consider a range of tests; i.e., walk tests, voltage variation, temperature and humidity, electromagnetic susceptibility, vibration, standby power, handling shock tests.

d. Functional Testing. A functional test, in conformance with the manufacturer's specification, should be performed prior to acceptance of the installed system and thereafter as determined necessary by the facility. An example of a functional test would be having an individual move at a rate of 1 foot(.30 meter) per second or faster within the sensor's total field of view and its plane of detection.

e. Performance Testing. Interior IDS must be performance tested in accordance with locally established procedures, (i.e., walking, running, jumping, crawling, or rolling along the path to the item being protected) at a documented frequency.

3. EXTERIOR IDS REQUIREMENTS.

a. Exterior IDS. Exterior IDSs must be designed, where economically feasible, with independent redundant data communication paths for protecting DOE S&S interests. The paths must be documented in an SSP or protection procedures, consistent with Table 1, Line Supervision Protection.

b. Detection Capability. The IDS must be capable of detecting an individual crossing the detection zone by walking, crawling, jumping, running, or rolling, or climbing the fence at any point in the detection zone, with a detection probability of 90 percent and confidence level of 95 percent.

   (1) The IDS must be tested when installed and annually (at least every 12 months) thereafter to validate that it meets detection probability and confidence level requirements.

   (2) Any time the IDS falls below the required probability of detection, the IDS must be repaired and retested.

   (3) When calculating detection probability for multiple sensor technology systems, detection is assumed if any of the sensors/zones report an intrusion. Multiple sensor technology systems may include taut wire, microwave, infra-red, ported coax, and laser components.

c. Miscellaneous Openings. For all openings in exterior barriers, unattended gates and/or entry/exit points, culverts and sewers, that meet the unattended opening criteria of Chapter VI, intrusion detection capabilities must be as effective as the rest of the perimeter IDS.

d. Perimeter Alarm/Detection and Assessment System. Perimeter Alarm/Detection and Assessment systems must be:

   (1) designed to cover the entire perimeter without a gap in detection, including the sides and tops of buildings situated within;

(2)   located such that the length of each detection zone is consistent with the characteristics of the sensors used in that zone and the topography;designed, installed, and maintained to deter adversaries from circumventing the detection system;provided with an isolation zone at least 20 feet (6 meters) wide and clear of fabricated or natural objects that would interfere with operation of detection systems or the effectiveness of the assessment;

(5)   free of wires, piping, poles, and similar objects that could be used to assist an intruder traversing the isolation zone or that could assist in the undetected ingress or egress of an adversary or matter; and

(6)   constructed in a manner that detects and deters the use of wire, piping, poles, etc., that cannot be eliminated from the isolation zone.

e.   Alarm Zone Degradation. Each alarm zone must be kept free of snow, ice, grass, weeds, debris, wildlife, and any other item that may degrade the effectiveness of the system. When this cannot be accomplished and detection capabilities become degraded, compensatory measures are required.

4.   RADIO FREQUENCY ALARM COMMUNICATIONS. Radio frequency alarm communications are appropriate when used for the protection of government property and classified matter. RF communications may also be used in the protection of S&S interests in emergency and temporary situations. In addition RF may be used as part of a site's early warning system. The use of RF communications in the protection of SNM in other than a temporary or emergency situation are described in the appendices of this manual. An IDS may use radio frequency communications to transmit alarm and other data for alarms, video, and other data utilized by the IDS provided:

a.   The data being transmitted are not classified.

b.   The data being transmitted are protected consistent with the program office cyber security plan and DOE requirements (see Chapter 9, DOE M 200.1-1, *Telecommunications Security Manual*, dated 2-15-00).

5.   PROTECTION OF IDSs.

a.   General Requirements.

(1)   IDS equipment should be protected in a graded manner consistent with the security interest being protected.

(2)   System components protecting Top Secret, and vital equipment SCIF and SAPF activities must be protected with tamper indication in both the access and the secure modes. Tamper indication is required for intrusion detection/alarm devices. Tamper switch wiring must be as listed below.

        (a)   Communication links, field processors and associated equipment must be provided with tamper detection switches on enclosure covers wired to a 24-hour circuit. The wiring must be protected from unauthorized access per UL Standard 681.

        (b)   All tamper switches (e.g., senors, processors, cable terminal boxes, control units, etc.) must be wired into a 24-hour circuit. More than one switch may be wired to a single circuit if the switches are located in the same general area.

        (c)   The switches may be wired as part of the line supervision circuit per UL Standard 681. However, tamper switches may be wired independent of line supervision circuits for hazardous areas, radiological controlled areas, SNM storage vaults, and other areas where testing and maintenance cost would be offset by using a separate circuit.

    (3)   Commercial Central Alarm Station Service firms must issue a current Underwriter's Laboratory (UL) certification commensurate with the contracted service and must maintain this UL certification as long as the service is provided to the facility. For the protection of classified matter UL 2050, National Industrial Security Service standard, should be implemented and a certificate issued for compliance with the UL standard. For other non-classified matter situations, Proprietary Burglar-Alarm Units and Systems- UL 1076, should be implemented and a certificate issued for compliance with the UL standard.

  b.   <u>Enclosures and Junction Boxes</u>. Permanent junction boxes, field distribution boxes, cable terminal boxes, and cabinets (equipment that terminates, splices, and groups interior or exterior IDS input or that could allow tampering, spoofing, bypassing, or other system sabotage) must be afforded tamper protection. When a box is secured by a Level IV locking device, the keys may be master keyed. Tamper switches must provide a tamper indication to the annunciators. Manholes and other enclosures, if serving as a junction box for data communication cables, must be protected from unauthorized access.

  c.   <u>Line Supervision</u>. Line supervision is required for IDSs protecting S&S interests. For property protection areas, line supervision may be provided consistent with a documented cost/benefit analysis as determined by the cognizant security authority. Where data encryption is used, key changes must be made annually (at least every 12 months) and whenever compromise is suspected. The requirements for line supervision are listed in Table 3, Line Supervision Protection.

    (1)   Line Supervision Options. Different combinations of line supervision are allowed depending on link routing:

(a)   An alarm communication link remaining within the security area and alarm communication link going through a lower security area.

(b)   Line supervision is required for the two primary segments of alarm data transmission: from sensor to data gathering panel (DGP)/field processor and from DGP/field processor to DGP/field processor or the central processing unit.

(2)   Classes of Line Supervision. Performance-based definitions are listed below in descending order of protection.

(a)   In general, Classes A through C apply to alarm communication links between data gathering panels/field processors, between data gathering panels/field processors and central alarm computers or alarm annunciator panels, and between computers.

1   For Class A, the data transmission must comply with DOE requirements (see Chapter 9, DOE M 200.1-1, *Telecommunications Security Manual*, dated 2-15-00).

2   For Class B, data must be transmitted by one of the following:

a   encryption using a proprietary encryption scheme that results in non-repetitive communications,

b   pseudo-random polling scheme,

c   non-encryption over fiber optic cable enclosed in conduit, or

d   non-encryption over fiber optic cable monitored by an optical supervision system.

3   For Class C, unencrypted data transmissions include:

a   RS-232, RS-485, etc., data transmission standard;

b   standard repetitive polling schemes; and

c   exception reporting with repetitive polling for health checks.

(b)   Classes D through F apply to data transmission through changes in the analog signal. In general, Classes D through F apply to alarm communication links between a sensor and a field processor.

    <u>1</u>   Class D supervision must combine various frequencies of alternating current (AC), be pulsed direct current (DC) or be a combination of AC and DC.

    <u>2</u>   Class E supervision must be an AC signal.

    <u>3</u>   Class F supervision must be a DC signal.

(3)   Protecting Alarm Wiring. Physical protection of alarm wiring must be as listed below.

    (a)   Protection for communication links must meet the requirements for the National Electric Code for protection from damage (see UL Standard 681).

    (b)   Protection for wiring between the sensor and the field processor using Class F line supervision must be protected from access. For alarm wiring protecting Top Secret, and vital equipment, protection for wiring between the sensor and the DGP/field processor using Class F line supervision must be protected from access when the DGP/field processor is outside the area being protected. Acceptable methods for protecting alarm system wiring are as follows:

        <u>1</u>   a totally concealed or embedded conduit system;

        <u>2</u>   junction boxes, pull boxes and other openings sealed by welding, epoxy-sealed threads, locked cover plates, tamper-resistant screws, or tamper alarm switches;

        <u>3</u>   alarm coverage of all wiring; or

        <u>4</u>   armored cable/wire or threaded conduit.

d.   <u>Alarm Annunciation and Response.</u>

(1)   Line supervision alarms Classes A through C must annunciate in both the CAS and the SAS indicating the type of alarm (data error, loss of communication, tamper, etc.) and the affected equipment.

(2)   Sensor to DGP/field processor (Classes C through F) line supervision alarms must annunciate in both the CAS and SAS, indicating the sensor or sensors affected.

(3)   PF personnel must be put on alert, and system maintenance personnel must be notified, when line supervision alarms indicate a loss of a communications path of a redundant system.

(4)   Line supervision alarm, tamper alarm, or radio frequency alarm events (e.g., "statement-of-health" alarm, sensor alarm, tamper alarm, and radio frequency jamming indications) must be treated the same as an intrusion alarm for the area being protected.

(5)   Maintenance personnel must be notified of a tamper or line supervision alarm, and the alarm condition must be assessed by PF response personnel.

(a)   Compensatory measures must be implemented to protect the alarmed location until required testing and repairs are completed.

(b)   Tamper and line supervision alarms must be tested to verify effectiveness. Alarm system components being protected by the tamper alarm, e.g., BMS, microwave, passive infrared, must be tested through physical actuation (see Table 1. Line Supervision Protection).

Table 1. Line Supervision Protection

Communication Lines between a Field Processor and Field Processor or a Central Processor				
	Vital Equipment or Top Secret Classified Matter	Classified Matter Secret and below	Maximum Internal System communications supervision interval	Required Manual Testing
	Class of Supervision	Class of Supervision	(ALL)	(ALL)
Routed within the alarm area	C	C	15 Minutes	Annually*
Routed through a lower security area	B	C	10 minutes	Annually*
Routed through an unsecured area	A	B	5 minutes	Annually*
Wiring from the Sensor to the Data Gathering Panel (DGP)				
All field wiring	F	F	Continuously	Annually*

*At least every 12 months

6.   ELECTRICAL POWER. Electrical power to supply the intrusion detection and assessment systems should be provided to assure continuous system availability and operation. The scope of the primary and auxiliary power sources are as follows.

a.   Primary Power. All IDS must have primary power from normal onsite power. The power source must contain a switching capability for component and total system testing. This testing can be used to determine the capacity and source of the required auxiliary power. The following system elements should be considered in configuring the power requirements.

        (1)   Alarm and communication systems should receive primary power directly from the onsite power distribution system. When the facility does not receive its power from an internal distribution system, power would come directly from the public utility.

        (2)   Alarm control panels, alarm management systems and automated information systems or associated critical components must be connected to an uninterruptible power supply or auxiliary power.

    b.   Auxiliary-Uninterruptible Power. Auxiliary or uninterruptible power sources should be provided for alarm systems requiring continuous power and for systems that, if interrupted, would degrade or compromise the protection afforded the asset.

7.   ASSESSMENT OF IDS ALARMS. An effective method must be established for assessing IDS alarms (e.g., line supervision, intrusion, false, nuisance, system failures, tamper, and radio frequency when radio frequency is used).

    a.   Alarms must be assessed immediately by either the PF or by a central alarm monitoring station personnel using CCTV.

    b.   CCTV assessment cameras used as primary assessment for alarms should be fixed (i.e., not pan or tilt) with fixed focal length lenses or may have a zoom capability.

CHAPTER X. ENTRY/EXIT SCREENING

1. GENERAL. With the exception of Protected and Material Access areas where inspection is mandatory, random inspections are to be conducted at other designated security boundaries. The cognizant security authority must determine the locations and scope of a screening program at other than PA and MA boundaries. An inspection program must be configured to detected prohibited and controlled articles before being brought into DOE facilities. These programs are to protect Department assets and interests from unauthorized removal without management authorization. Any entry/exit inspection program must be documented in an SSP or procedure.

    a. Passage of individuals, vehicles, and/or packages or mail through entry control point inspection equipment must be observed and controlled by trained designated personnel.

    b. Inspection equipment can include handheld and/or portable detectors, metal detectors, special nuclear material detectors, explosive detectors, and x-ray systems and must assist security personnel in ensuring that prohibited and controlled articles will be detected before being brought into or removed from DOE facilities.

    c. Entrance inspections of personnel, vehicles, packages, and hand-carried items must be performed to deter and detect prohibited and controlled articles. Formally established inspection rates are to be issued by the cognizant security authority.

        (1) Bypass routes around inspection equipment must be closed or monitored to deter unauthorized passage of personnel and hand-carried articles.

        (2) Uninterrupted power must be provided to all inspection equipment. In those instances where uninterruptable power is not practical, there must be locally developed procedures to provide alternative measures for conducting entry/exit screening when loss of electrical power occurs.

        (3) Measures are to be instituted to correctly maintain control settings on all entry/exit control point inspection equipment.

        (4) Equipment, to include portal monitors, must have audible and visual alarms monitored by on-post trained personnel.

        (5) Ingress/egress points must be designed to preclude commingling of searched and unsearched personnel.

2. ENTRY/EXIT INSPECTIONS.

    a. Explosives Detection.

        (1) Sites must analyze their facilities to determine the potential for an adversary to use explosives to affect consequences such as sabotage or

theft of DOE assets or fatalities and show that sufficient protective measures have been implemented to result in a low risk of a successful attack. Protective measures may include the integration of various technologies, screening of people, packages, and vehicles as well as the hardening of facilities and other assets to be able to withstand an attack from explosives. This analysis must be included in the overall protection planning process (see DOE M 470.4-1).

(2)   If the analysis determines that explosive detection is required, explosive detection equipment must ensure that explosives are not introduced without appropriate authorization. The SSP or procedure must document the analysis that establishes a facility's capability to detect explosives and provide protection against the malicious use of explosives.

(3)   Documentation must include the rationale for explosive detection equipment/systems selection, deployment, and use.

(4)   Security personnel procedures for explosive detection equipment must be approved by the cognizant security authority.

b.   Metal Detection must be used in the entry process at designated security area boundaries. The cognizant security authority must designate the protected area location for the conduct of the screening.

(1)   Metal detectors must ensure weapons are not introduced without authorization.

(2)   Metal detectors used for protected area entry inspection must detect test weapons listed in Chapter V.

(3)   The site must implement the performance testing procedures and test objects or the standards cited in Chapter V.

c.   X-ray Machines may be used to supplement metal detectors and protective personnel hand searches for prohibited and controlled articles. X-ray machines must provide a discernable image of the prohibited and controlled article (see Chapter V).

d.   SNM Detectors used in the inspection process must ensure SNM is not removed without authorization. SNM detectors used in the inspection process must be tested using trace elements that depict the type of material located within the security area. The thresholds must be consistent with the SNM type, form, quantity, attractiveness level, size, configuration, portability, and credible diversion amounts of the articles or property contained within the area.

e.   Personnel, Vehicles, and Hand-Carried Items including packages, briefcases, purses, and lunch containers are to be inspected to deter and detect unauthorized removal of classified matter or other safeguards and security interests from designated security areas.

(1) Explosive vapor detectors and metal detectors should be used in a combination that precludes the opportunity to defeat the detectors individually at designated area boundaries and when used to inspect personnel for explosives or other prohibited/controlled articles.

(2) Metal detectors used in the exit inspection process must ensure shielded material is not removed without authorization.

(3) Specific inspection procedures and response to alarms with limitations and thresholds for the various detectors must be established and documented in the SSP or procedure.

(4) Exit inspection procedures must be written to ensure:

    (a) The identification of detection thresholds for the various specified threats and shielding. The thresholds must be consistent with the type, form, quantity, attractiveness level, size, configuration, portability, and credible diversion amounts of material contained within the area.

    (b) The conduct of random exit inspections at a facility boundary, when a site perimeter boundary encompasses a sensitive area. The frequency must be determined by DOE line management.

f. <u>Entry Control Point Systems</u> must allow the authorized entry and exit of personnel while detecting prohibited and controlled articles. Entry control point configuration must have separate material package inspection areas/stations for inspecting personnel, packages, and hand-carried items. The following design criteria apply:

(1) Entry/exit point inspection monitors must be collocated with designated security posts to facilitate the initiation of a response to an alarm.

(2) Security posts must be designed with an unobstructed view to facilitate observation of any attempt to bypass systems.

(3) Security structures should consider the requirements in Appendix B.

(4) Entrances/exits must be alarmed with intrusion detection sensors or controlled at all times to notify of unauthorized use.

APPENDIX A. PROTECTION OF CATEGORY III AND IV SPECIAL NUCLEAR MATERIAL

This Appendix contains the physical protection requirements for Category III and IV quantities of special nuclear material. These requirements are in addition to those physical protection requirements outlined in the base CRD.

CHAPTER A-I. PROTECTION OF
CATEGORY III AND IV SPECIAL NUCLEAR MATERIAL

1. GENERAL REQUIREMENTS. This Appendix contains the requirements for protecting Category III and IV quantities of special nuclear material (SNM). The priority of protection measures must be designed to prevent malevolent acts such as theft, diversion, and radiological sabotage and to respond to adverse conditions such as emergencies caused by acts of nature.

    a. A facility must not possess, receive, process, transport, or store SNM until that facility has been cleared (see DOE M 470.4-1, *Safeguards and Security Program Planning and Management*, dated 8-26-05).

    b. Physical protection for each category of SNM must consider the following factors: quantities, chemical forms, and isotopic composition purities; ease of separation, accessibility, concealment, portability; radioactivity; and self-protecting features (see DOE M 470.4-6 Chg 1, and 10 CFR Part 73, Physical Protection Plants and Materials, relative to self-protecting).

    c. The protection of nuclear material production, reactors, and fuel must be commensurate with the category of SNM.

    d. SNM, parts, or explosives that are classified must receive the physical protection required by the higher level of classification or category of SNM, whichever is the more stringent.

2. CATEGORY III QUANTITIES OF SNM. The following requirements apply.

    a. In Use or Processing. Category III quantities of SNM must be used or processed in an access controlled security area within at least a limited area (LA) and in accordance with local security procedures approved by the DOE cognizant security authority.

    b. Storage. Category III quantities of SNM must be stored within a locked security container or room, either of which must be located within at least an LA. The container or room must be under the protection of an intrusion detection system or protective force patrol physical check at least every 8 hours.

3. CATEGORY IV QUANTITIES OF SNM. The following requirements apply.

    a. In Use or Processing. Category IV quantities of SNM must be used or processed within at least a property protection area and in accordance with local security procedures approved by the DOE cognizant security authority.

    b. Storage. Category IV quantities of SNM must be stored in a locked area within at least a property protection area, and procedures must be documented in an approved SSP.

4.   <u>LIMITED AREAS</u>. LAs are security areas that are established to protect classified matter and Category III quantities of SNM and to serve as a concentric layer of protection. In addition to the requirements for a PPA, the following apply to an LA.

    a.   <u>General Requirements</u>. LAs are defined by physical barriers encompassing the designated space and access controls to ensure that only authorized personnel are allowed to enter the area.

    b.   <u>Access Control</u>. Access controls must be in place to ensure that only appropriately cleared and authorized personnel are permitted unescorted access to the LA. Access must be based on an individual's need-to-know to perform official duties, validation of the individual's security clearance, and the presentation of a DOE security badge. Access must be controlled when going from one security area into another security area with increased protection requirements. Where practical, automated access control systems must be used in place of PF or other authorized personnel to control access into security areas.

        (1)   If automated access control equipment is used, a DOE security badge must be used to access electronically stored information relevant to the badge and badge holder.

        (2)   Entry control points for vehicle and pedestrian access to security areas must provide the same level of protection as that provided at all other points along the security perimeter.

        (3)   Entry control points must be structurally hardened to meet site-specific criteria as documented in the SSP.

        (4)   Exits from security areas must satisfy life safety requirements of National Fire Protection Association (NFPA) 101, *Safety to Life from Fire in Buildings and Structures.* Some exits may be provided for emergency use only.

        (5)   Security area entrances and exits must be equipped with doors, gates, rails, or other movable barriers that direct and control the movement of personnel or vehicles through designated control points.

        (6)   Door locks and latches used on security area perimeters must meet life safety requirements of NFPA 101.

        (7)   Automated gates must be designed to allow manual operation during power outages or mechanism failures. Where automated gates are used to control vehicular access to a security area, the gates and openings must be constructed to permit operation from a monitoring/control point or from other manned security posts.

(8)   Site-specific requirements and procedures for visitor logs must be approved by the cognizant security authority. If visitor logs are to be used at the PPA, the requirements set forth in Chapter II of this CRD are to be followed.

c.   <u>Personnel Access</u>.Escort Ratios. The cognizant security authority must establish escort-to-visitor ratios in a graded manner for each security area.

(2)   Escort Responsibilities. Any person permitted to enter a security area who does not possess a security clearance at the appropriate level must be escorted at all times by an appropriately cleared and knowledgeable individual trained in local escort procedures.

(a)   Escorts must ensure measures are taken to prevent compromise of S&S interests.

(b)   The escort must ensure the visitor has a need-to-know for the security area or the S&S interests.

(3)   Access Validation. Validation must occur at LA entry control points.

(a)   The identity and security clearance held by each person seeking entry must be validated by appropriately authorized personnel, automated systems, or other means documented in the SSP.

(b)   Where practicable, PF personnel will not be used to control access to LAs.

(4)   "Piggybacking." The following requirements must be documented in the SSP if piggybacking into LAs is permitted.

(a)   Personnel with the appropriate security clearance may vouch for another person with the required security clearance to "piggyback" into an LA.

(b)   Authorized personnel permitting the entry of another person must inspect the individual's DOE security badge to ensure that it bears a likeness of the individual and that he or she has identified, by badge marking, the proper security clearance. Authorized individuals entering an LA, when PF personnel are not controlling access, are responsible and must ensure that unauthorized individuals do not enter ("piggyback").

(5)   Automated Access Control Systems. Automated access control systems may be used if the following requirements are met.

(a)   Automated access controls used for access to a security area must verify that the security clearance and the DOE security badge are valid (i.e., that the badge data read by the system match the data assigned to the badge holder). Badges may be validated by means of a personal identification number (PIN) or other approved means as stipulated in the SSP.

(b) When remote, unattended, automated access control system entry control points are used for access to security areas, the barrier must be resistant to bypass. The unattended entry control point should have closed-circuit television system coverage.

(c) Automated control system alarms (e.g., annunciation of a door alarm, duress alarm, tamper alarm, or anti-passback indication feature) must be treated as an intrusion alarm for the area being protected.

(d) Personnel or other protective measures are required to protect PINs, card reader access transactions, displays (e.g., badge-encoded data), and keypad devices. The process of inputting, storing, displaying, or recording verification data must ensure the data are protected in accordance with the SSP.

(e) The system must record all attempts at access to include unsuccessful, unauthorized, and authorized.

(f) Door locks opened by badge readers must be designed to relock immediately after the door has closed.

(g) Transmission lines that carry security clearance and personal identification or verification data between devices/equipment must be protected in accordance with the SSP.

(h) Records reflecting active assignments of DOE security badges, PINs, security clearance, and similar system-related records must be maintained. Records of personnel removed from the system must be retained for 1 year, unless a longer period is specified by other requirements. Personal data must be protected (See 5 U.S.C. 552a).

(i) Badge reader boxes, control lines, and junction boxes should have line supervision or tamper indication or be equipped with tamper-resistant devices. Field processors or multiplexers and other similar equipment must be tamper-alarmed or secured by a means that precludes surreptitious tampering with the equipment.

(j) Uninterrupted power supply or compensatory measures must be provided at installations where continuous operation is required.

(6)   Vehicle Access.

    (a)   DOE cognizant security authority approval for non-Government vehicles, which includes privately owned, to access LAs must be documented in the SSP. Additional factors to be considered are navigation systems, vehicle mounted back-up cameras, computers and cell phones.

    (b)   Government-owned or -leased vehicles may be admitted only when on official business and only when operated by properly cleared and authorized drivers or when the drivers are escorted by properly cleared and authorized personnel.

    (c)   The SSP must identify procedures for inspection of, and access by, service and delivery vehicles.

    (d)   All personnel within a vehicle are required to produce DOE security badges when accessing an LA.

    (e)   When a remote automated access control system is used for vehicle access control, it must verify that the operator or the escort has a valid DOE security badge (e.g., the badge data read by the system must match the data assigned to the badge holder) and a valid security clearance.

d.   Emergency Personnel and Vehicles. Emergency personnel and vehicles may be authorized for immediate entry to the LA in response to an emergency if conditions and procedures for immediate entry are documented in the SSP.

(1)   If the emergency condition prevents an exit inspection before departing the site, an escort must be provided, and both personnel and emergency vehicles must be inspected as soon as the emergency is over. If an escort is not provided, provisions must be made for continuous surveillance of all emergency vehicles that enter the LA.

(2)   As described in DOE M 470.4-4A, *Information Security*, dated 1-16-09, local procedures must be developed for safeguarding classified matter from inadvertent access, by uncleared personnel, or cleared persons who do not have a need-to-know, during emergencies.

e.   Inspection Program. Entry/exit inspections are required to ensure that prohibited and controlled articles are not introduced without authorization. Likewise such programs must ensure S&S interests are not removed from DOE facilities. Application of entry/exit inspections at locations other than PA and MA boundaries is at the discretion of DOE line management. This discretion extends to security areas containing Category III and IV SNM. The inspection process and locations where inspections are to be conducted must be documented in the

SSP. Consideration should be given to conducting these inspections before entry to an LA and after exit from an LA. An inspection program must be established by the cognizant security authority and documented in the SSP.

    f.   <u>Intrusion Detection</u>. A determination should be made as to the application of electronic physical protection systems. The scope and configuration of these systems are described in Chapter IX. <u>Signs</u>. Signs must be posted to convey information on the Atomic Weapons and Special Nuclear Materials Rewards Act (P.L. 84-165, as amended by P.L. 93-377); prohibited and controlled articles; the inspection of vehicles, packages, hand-carried items, and persons entering or exiting the security area; the use of video surveillance equipment; and trespassing (see 42 U.S.C. Section 2278a).

5.   <u>EXCLUSION AREAS (EAs)</u>. EAs are security areas that are established to protect classified matter where an individual's mere presence may result in access to classified matter. In addition to requirements for an LA, the following apply to an EA.

    a.   <u>General Requirements</u>. The boundaries of EAs must be encompassed by physical barriers and be located within the minimum of an LA.

    b.   <u>Access Control</u>. In addition to the requirements for an LA the following requirements apply to access to an EA:

        (1)   Individuals permitted unescorted access must have the appropriate access authorizations and a need-to-know consistent with the classified matter to which they have access by virtue of their presence in the EA.

        (2)   Individuals without the appropriate security clearance and need-to-know must be escorted by a knowledgeable individual who must ensure measures are taken to prevent compromise of classified matter.

        (3)   Visitor logs must be used for EAs, PAs, and MAAs.

    c.   <u>Intrusion Detection</u>.

        (1)   Unauthorized entry into the EA must be detected.

        (2)   When the exclusion area is unoccupied, and classified matter is not secured in a security container, then the EA must at a minimum, meet the requirements of a vault-type room (VTR).

CHAPTER A-II. ALARM MANAGEMENT AND CONTROL SYSTEM

1. GENERAL REQUIREMENTS. This chapter establishes requirements for integrated physical protection systems protecting Category III SNM and if used for Category IV SNM. When intrusion detection system (IDS) sensors are used to protect safeguards and security (S&S) interests the sensors must annunciate directly to alarm stations when an alarm is activated.

2. ALARM STATIONS. Alarm stations must provide a capability for monitoring and assessing alarms and initiating responses to S&S events.

    a. Alarm station personnel must be knowledgeable of the area being protected and the emergency notification procedures. Knowledge of the area does not encompass the operations contained therein or what is stored or processed. As an example, area knowledge would involve the building alarm configuration, room numbers within the structure, pedestrian and vehicle entry points, etc.

    b. Tamper and supervisory alarms must be assessed by authorized personnel and technical/maintenance support personnel in accordance with local procedures.

    c. Alarm stations must indicate the status of the systems and annunciate a status change. The system must indicate the type and location of the alarm.

    d. Records must be kept of each alarm received in the alarm station and of any maintenance activities conducted on the alarm system or any of the related components.

    e. Personnel manning the alarm station must possess an appropriate security clearance (i.e., Q or L) commensurate with the most sensitive interest under the protection of the alarm station.

    f. Access control systems must ensure admission of authorized personnel only.

    g. Alarms must annunciate both audibly and visibly to an alarm station.

    h. Multiple alarms must be prioritized based on the importance of the S&S interests.

3. COMMERCIAL CENTRAL ALARM STATIONS. Commercial alarm service firm must issue a current Underwriter's Laboratory (UL) certification commensurate with the contracted service and must maintain this UL certification as long as the service is provided to the facility. For the protection of the classified matter, UL 2050, National Industrial Security Service standards, should be implemented and a certificate issued for compliance with the UL standard.

CHAPTER A-III. INTRUSION DETECTION AND ASSESSMENT SYSTEMS

1. <u>PROTECTING SPECIAL NUCLEAR MATERIAL</u>. Intrusion detection and assessment systems and/or visual observations by protective force (PF) personnel must be used to protect SNM and classified matter to ensure breaches of security barriers or boundaries are detected and alarms annunciate. The following requirements apply for alarms protecting Category III, and when used for protecting Category IV quantities of SNM. Intrusion detection and assessment must be conducted in accordance with the site security plan. Appendix C, *Safeguards and Security Alarm Management and Control Systems* describes technical approaches for the employment of intrusion detection and alarm systems.

2. <u>INTERIOR INTRUSION DETECTION SYSTEM</u>. When used to protect either Category of SNM, IDSs must be configured to:

    a. detect unauthorized access to Category III and IV quantities of SNM;

    b. be compatible with other interior and exterior alarm devices and systems;

    c. automatically activate an alarm to notify of a changed security condition;

    d. function effectively in all environmental conditions;

    e. provide alarm communication line supervision;

    f. provide tamper protection on all alarm devices and alarm data gathering panels;,

    g. have a false and nuisance alarm rate as described in Chapter IX of this CRD, while maintaining proper detection sensitivity; and

    h. report alarm conditions to a dedicated location that facilitates continuous monitoring by designated, trained PF or security personnel.

3. <u>EXTERIOR IDS</u>. When used for either Category of SNM, exterior IDSs must be configured to:

    a. detect unauthorized access to Category III and IV quantities of SNM;

    b. compliment the interior IDS;

    c. automatically activate an alarm to notify of a changed security condition;

    d. function effectively in all environmental conditions;

    e. provide alarm communication line supervision;

    f. provide tamper protection on all alarm devices and alarm data gathering panels;

g.   have a false and nuisance alarm rate as described in Chapter IX of this CRD, while maintaining proper detection sensitivity;

h.   report alarm conditions to a dedicated location which facilitates continuous monitoring and assessment by designated trained PF or security administrative personnel; and

i.   The cognizant security authority develops the FAR/NAR standards based on site specific systems to achieve a Low As Responsible Achievable (ALARA) levels.

4.   <u>ASSESSMENT SYSTEMS</u>. An alarm assessment system allows security personnel to determine rapidly whether an intrusion has taken place at a remote location. When used, assessment systems must be configured as an element of the total IDS along with the required complimentary lighting.

    a.   A basic assessment system is composed of CCTV cameras positioned at strategic points covering the intrusion detection devices/zones, video display monitors located at a central location, and various transmission and switching systems connecting CCTV cameras to monitors and video recording devices.

    b.   The lighting must allow for the fast and reliable assessment of alarms from either the CCTV system or PF personnel as defined in the SSP.

5.   <u>PERFORMANCE TESTING</u>. Systems and system elements are to be performance tested at a documented frequency (see DOE M 470.4-1). The testing program must be implemented in locally prepared planning or procedural documents.

6.   <u>MAINTENANCE</u>. Corrective maintenance procedures for supporting security related systems and subsystems protecting Category III and IV quantities of SNM, must be approved by line management and prescribed in the site's operation procedures.

    a.   A scope to preparing corrective maintenance procedures can be found in Chapter V of the base manual.

    b.   Preventative maintenance must be performed on critical systems, subsystems and components in conformance with manufacturer's specifications and/or local procedures.

    c.   Maintenance personnel must be notified of a tamper or line supervisions alarm, and the alarm condition must be assessed by PF response personnel.

    d.   Tamper and line supervision alarms must be tested to verify effectiveness. BMS, microwave, passive infrared, buried line sensors and DGP/alarm processing panels, must be tested through physical activation of the switch (see Table A-1, Line Supervision Protection).

Table A-1. Line Supervision Protection

	Cat I or II SNM,	Cat III or IV SNM, Classified Matter Secret and below	Maximum Internal System communications supervision interval	Required Manual Testing
Communication Lines between a Field Processor and Field Processor or a Central Processor				
	Class of Supervision	Class of Supervision	(ALL)	(ALL)
Routed within the alarm area	C	C	15 Minutes	Annually*
Routed through a lower security area	B	C	10 minutes	Annually*
Routed through an unsecured area	A	B	5 minutes	Annually*
Wiring from the Sensor to the Data Gathering Panel (DGP)				
All field wiring	F	F	Continuously	Annually*

*At least every 12 months

CHAPTER A-IV. COMMUNICATIONS

1. RADIO FREQUENCY ALARM COMMUNICATIONS FOR INTRUSION DETECTION SYSTEMS. IDS may use wireless radio frequency communications to transmit alarm and other data for alarms, video, early warning devices, and other data utilized by the IDS provided:

   a. The data being transmitted are not classified.

   b. The data being transmitted are protected consistent with the program office cyber security plan and DOE requirements (see Chapter 9, DOE M 200.1-1, *Telecommunications Security Manual*, dated 2-15-00).

2. OTHER REQUIREMENTS. Radio frequency communications for IDS must also meet the following requirements.

   a. Provide self-checking alarm communication paths that annunciate system failure in the alarm stations.

   b. Ensure that the statement-of-health interval allows for an assessment and response.

   c. Provide unique status change messages for alarm, tamper, and power conditions.

   d. Provide an operator-initiated polling feature to allow a check of communication link integrity.

   e. Have tamper-resistant or tamper-switch alarm transmitters.

   f. Have auxiliary power for critical components until power can be restored or compensatory measures can be implemented.

   g. Not produce spurious signals that interfere with other security system components.

   h. Provide a unique electronic address code for each transmitter/receiver pair.

   i. Provide a means of interfacing to the alarm annunciation system (e.g., the alarm station or central alarm station).

   j. Provide reliable communications in all weather conditions.

   k. Ensure system integrity is maintained (i.e., not diminished) during multiple alarms.

   l. Operate on authorized frequency bands.

m.   Not change status on a network; e.g., from secure mode to access mode (if the status of the network is changed, the alarm system operator must be advised of the mode change).

n.   Be performance-tested in accordance with established performance assurance procedures at a documented frequency (see DOE M 470.4-1).

3.   <u>RISK ASSESSMENT</u>. If conducted a risk assessment must be documented. The conclusion must be that the risk is acceptable and in the best interests of the Government to accept it (based on a decision by the cognizant security authority).

CHAPTER A-V. PROTECTION DURING TRANSPORTATION

1. GENERAL REQUIREMENTS. This chapter defines requirements for the transportation of Category III and IV SNM. Category III quantities of SNM may be transported by the following methods unless otherwise prohibited by statute (see DOE O 460.2A, *Departmental Materials Transportation and Packaging Management*, dated 12-22-04). Other items of special national security interests may, on occasion, be designated for transportation safeguards system transport (see DOE O 461.1A, *Packaging and Transfer or Transportation of Materials of National Security Interest*, dated 4-26-04). Classified nuclear explosive parts, components, special assemblies, sub-critical test devices, trainers or shapes containing no fissile nuclear material or less than Category II quantities of fissile nuclear material must be shipped consistent with both DOE policy governing protection of classified information and Department of Transportation regulations governing interstate transportation.

2. CATEGORY III QUANTITIES OF SNM. Offsite shipments of Category III quantities of SNM may be transported by the following authorized methods unless otherwise prohibited by statute (see DOE O 460.2A).

    a. Domestic offsite shipments of classified configurations of Category III quantities of SNM must be made by Office of Secure Transportation (OST) or by an OST-approved commercial carrier that meets the requirements listed in paragraph 2a(1)(a) below.

    b. Offsite shipments of unclassified configurations of Category III quantities of SNM are not required to be made by OST. If OST is not used, the shipments may be made by the following means:

        (1) Truck or Train Shipment. The following requirements must be met.

            (a) Government-owned or exclusive-use truck, commercial carrier, or rail may be used.

            (b) Transport vehicles must be inspected by security personnel before loading and shipment. Cargo compartments must be locked and sealed after the inspection and remain sealed while en route.

            (c) Shipment escorts must periodically communicate with a control station operator. The control station operator must be capable of requesting appropriate local law enforcement agency response if needed.

            (d) No intermediate stops are permitted except for emergencies, driver relief, meals, refueling, or transfer of security interests.

(2) Air Shipment. Shipments must be under the direct observation of the authorized escorts during all land movements and loading and unloading operations.

c. Movement between security areas at the same site must comply with the locally developed and approved shipment security plan.

3. CATEGORY IV QUANTITIES OF SNM. Category IV quantities of SNM may be transported by the following methods unless otherwise prohibited by statute.

a. Domestic offsite shipments of classified configurations of Category IV quantities of SNM may be made by the OST or by other means when approved by DOE line management.

b. Shipments of unclassified Category IV quantities of SNM may be made by truck, rail, air, or water craft in commercial for-hire or leased vehicles. Shippers are required to give the consignee an estimated time of arrival before dispatch and to follow-up with a written confirmation not later than 48 hours after dispatch.

c. Consignees must promptly notify the shipper by telephone and written confirmation upon determination that a shipment has not arrived by the scheduled time. Upon initial notification, the shipper must report (see DOE M 470.4-1).

d. Shipments must be made by a mode of transportation that can be traced, and within 24 hours from request, can report on the last known location of the shipment should it fail to arrive on schedule.

APPENDIX B. PROTECTION OF NUCLEAR WEAPONS, COMPONENTS, AND CATEGORY I AND II SPECIAL NUCLEAR MATERIAL

This appendix contains the physical protection requirements for Category I and II quantities of special nuclear material. These requirements are in addition to those physical protection requirements outlined in the base CRD and Appendix A.

CHAPTER B-I. PROTECTION OF NUCLEAR WEAPONS, COMPONENTS, AND CATEGORY I AND II SPECIAL NUCLEAR MATERIAL

1. <u>GENERAL REQUIREMENTS</u>. This chapter defines requirements for protecting nuclear weapons, components, and Category I and II quantities of SNM. The priority of protection measures must be designed to prevent malevolent acts such as theft, diversion, and radiological sabotage and to respond to adverse conditions such as emergencies caused by acts of nature. SNM must be protected at the higher level when roll-up to Category I quantities can occur within a single security area unless the facility has conducted an analysis that determined roll up was not credible. The policy cited in this chapter applies to fixed facilities and sites within a designated Protected Area (PA) or Material Access Area (MAA) and not the conduct of onsite movement of SNM or operations managed by the Office of Secure Transportation (OST). The OST is responsible for the promulgation of specific internal guidance governing the protection afforded all DOE matter entrusted to OST for transport by surface and air. Transportation of SNM, whether onsite or by OST, must be provided protection equivalent to that provided by fixed sites for the same material.

    a. A facility must not possess, receive, process, transport, or store nuclear weapons or SNM until that facility has been cleared (see DOE M 470.4-1, *Safeguards and Security Program Planning and Management*, dated 8-26-05).

    b. An integrated system of positive measures must be developed and implemented to protect Category I and II quantities of SNM and nuclear weapons. Protection measures must address physical protection strategies of denial and containment as well as recapture, recovery, and/or pursuit.

    c. Physical protection for each category of SNM must consider the following factors: quantities, chemical forms, and isotopic composition purities; ease of separation, accessibility, concealment, portability; radioactivity; and self-protecting features (see DOE M 470.4-6 Chg 1, and 10 CFR Part 73, Physical Protection of Plants and Materials, relative to self-protecting).

    d. The protection of nuclear material production, reactors, and fuel must be commensurate with the category of SNM.

    e. SNM, parts, explosives or munitions that are classified must receive the physical protection required by the highest level of classification or category of SNM, whichever is the more stringent.

2. <u>CATEGORY I QUANTITIES OF SNM.</u>

    a. <u>In Use or Processing</u>. Category I quantities of SNM must be located within a material access area (MAA) inside a protected area (PA). Any MAA containing unattended Category I quantities of SNM must be equipped with an intrusion detection system or detection must be provided by protective force.<u>Storage</u>. Category I quantities of SNM must be stored within an MAA.Category I, attractiveness level A SNM must be stored in a vault. Storage facilities constructed after July 15, 1994 for Category I, attractiveness level A SNM must be underground or below grade.

(2)   Category I, attractiveness level B SNM must be stored in a vault or provided enhanced protection that exceeds vault-type room (VTR) storage (e.g., collocated with a protective force response station and/or activated barriers).

(3)   At a minimum Category I, attractiveness level C SNM must be stored in a VTR.

3.   <u>CATEGORY II QUANTITIES OF SNM</u>.

a.   <u>In Use or Processing</u>. Category II quantities of SNM must be located within a PA and under material surveillance procedures.

b.   <u>Storage</u>. Category II quantities of SNM must be stored in a vault or VTR located within a PA.

4.   <u>PROTECTED AREAS</u>. PAs are security areas typically located within an LA that are established to protect Category II or greater quantities of SNM and may also contain classified matter. The PA provides concentric layers of security for the MAA. In addition to meeting LA requirements, the following apply to a PA.

a.   <u>General Requirements</u>. PAs must be encompassed by physical barriers that identify the boundaries, surrounded by a perimeter intrusion detection and assessment system (PIDAS), and equipped with access controls that ensure only authorized personnel are allowed to enter and exit.

b.   <u>Inspection Program</u>. An inspection program must ensure prohibited and controlled articles are detected before being brought into PA facilities. All personnel, vehicles, packages, and hand-carried articles are subject to inspection before entry into a security area. Likewise, such programs must ensure S&S interest<u>s</u> are not removed. An inspection program must be established by the cognizant security authority and documented in the SSP.

c.   <u>Access Control.</u> When the PIN or biometric system is either not working or not implemented at security areas requiring measures in addition to access control (e.g., at a PA or MAA boundary), PF or other trained security personnel must perform the access control requirements as documented in the SSP.

(1)   Personnel Access.

(a)   Unescorted access must be controlled to limit entry to individuals with an L or Q security clearance.

(b)   Visitor logs must be used for PAs.

    (c)   Validation of the security clearance must occur at PA entry control points.

        <u>1</u>   The identity and security clearance of each person seeking entry must be validated by armed PF personnel or

        <u>2</u>   If PA access is controlled by an unattended automated access control system, the system must verify the following:

            <u>a</u>   a valid DOE security badge (badge validation must match the data assigned to the badge holder);

            <u>b</u>   valid security clearance; and

            <u>c</u>   valid PIN or

            <u>d</u>   valid biometric.

(2)   Vehicle Access.

    (a)   Private vehicles are prohibited.

    (b)   Government-owned or -leased vehicles may be admitted only when on official business and only when operated by properly cleared and authorized drivers or when the drivers are escorted by properly cleared and authorized personnel.

    (c)   Vendor vehicles are prohibited unless the vehicles and drivers have been subjected to a thorough inspection/investigation and been given access approval by the DOE cognizant security authority. As an alternative, provisions must be established for using trained escorts.

(3)   Entrance Inspections. Entrance inspections of all personnel, vehicles, packages, and hand-carried items must be performed to deter and detect prohibited and controlled articles.

    (a)   Bypass routes around inspection equipment must be closed or monitored to deter unauthorized passage of personnel and hand-carried articles.

    (b)   Uninterrupted power must be provided to all control point inspection equipment.

    (c)   Measures must be taken to preclude the unauthorized alteration of control settings on all entry/exit control point inspection equipment.

(d)   Equipment, to include portal monitors, must have both audible and visual alarms monitored by assigned PF personnel.

(e)   Ingress/egress points must be designed to preclude commingling of searched and unsearched personnel.

(f)   Passage of individuals, vehicles, and/or packages or mail through entry control point inspection equipment must be observed and controlled by PF personnel. Inspection equipment can include metal detectors, SNM detectors, explosive detectors, and x-ray systems and must ensure that prohibited and controlled articles specific for the PA are detected before being brought into DOE facilities. Hand-held and/or portable detectors, etc., must be available to resolve alarms and be available for use during inspection equipment failures.

(4)   Explosive Detection.

(a)   Sites must analyze their facilities to determine the potential for an adversary to use explosives to affect consequences and show that sufficient protective measures have been implemented to reduce the risk of a successful attack. The specific location of the screening will be determined by the cognizant security authority. In any instance it must be before gaining access to a PA. The scope of the protective measures are described in Chapter II of the base manual and supported by a risk analysis (see DOE M 470.4-1).

(b)   If the analysis determines that explosive detection is required, explosive detection equipment must ensure that explosives are not introduced without appropriate authorization. The SSP must document the analysis that establishes a facility's capability to detect explosives and provides protection against the malicious use of explosives.

(c)   Documentation must include the rationale for explosive detection equipment/systems selection, deployment, and use.

(5)   Metal Detection must be used in the entry process at all designated protected area boundaries.

(a)   Metal detectors must ensure prohibited and controlled articles are not introduced to designated protection areas without authorization.

(b)   Metal detectors used for entry inspection must detect test weapons listed in Chapter V.

        (c)   Metal detectors scheduled to be replaced after Fiscal Year 2010 must meet the performance testing procedures and objects cited in Section 5.1, 5.2 and portions of 5.3 relating to non-ferro-magnetic stainless knives cited in National Institute of Justice (NIJ) Standard 0601.02, *Law Enforcement and Corrections Standards and Testing Program* (see Chapter X).

    (6)   SNM Detectors. SNM detectors used in the inspection process must ensure SNM is not removed without authorization. The testing should provide for the identification of detection thresholds for the SNM type, form, quantity, attractiveness level, size, configuration, portability, and credible diversion amounts of articles or property contained within the area.

    (7)   Exit Inspections. Personnel, vehicles, and hand-carried items including packages, briefcases, purses, and lunch containers are to be inspected to deter and detect unauthorized removal of classified matter or other S&S interests from PAs. The cognizant security authority is to determine whether the inspections will be conducted at the PA or MAA. The determination will be documented in a SSP.

        (a)   SNM detectors and metal detectors must be used in a combination that precludes the opportunity to defeat the detectors individually and/or when used to inspect personnel for prohibited and controlled articles.

        (b)   Metal detectors used in the exit inspection process must ensure shielded SNM is not removed without authorization.

        (c)   Specific inspection procedures and the approach to responding to alarms with limitations and thresholds for SNM detectors must be established and documented in the SSP or a procedure.

        (d)   Exit inspection procedures must be written to ensure the following.

            <u>1</u>   Identification of detection thresholds for security interests. The thresholds must be consistent with the type, form, quantity, attractiveness level, size, configuration, portability, and credible diversion amounts of articles or property contained within the area.

            <u>2</u>   The detection of shielded SNM (e.g., by using entry control point screening system equipment in a combination that precludes the opportunity to defeat the detectors individually).

<u>3</u>   Entry control points without the means to detect unauthorized removal of material are not used to exit except in emergencies where equivalent protection searches are conducted at an assembly area).

<u>4</u>   Random exit inspections are conducted at facility boundaries. The frequency must be determined by DOE line management.

(8)   Entry and Exit Control Points. Entry control point systems must allow the authorized entry and exit of personnel while detecting prohibited and controlled articles. Entry control point design must include separate material package inspection stations for inspecting personnel, packages, and hand-carried items. The following design criteria apply.

(a)   Entry/exit point inspection monitors must be collocated with PF posts to facilitate the initiation of a response to an alarm.

(b)   Security posts must be designed with an unobstructed view to facilitate observation of any attempt to bypass systems.

(c)   Security structures must meet the requirements in Appendix B, Chapter VII of this CRD.

(d)   Entrances/exits must be equipped with intrusion detection sensors or controlled at all times.

5.   <u>MATERIAL ACCESS AREAS</u>. MAAs are security areas that are established to protect Category I quantities of SNM. In addition to requirements for a PA the following apply to an MAA.

a.   <u>General Requirements</u>. MAAs must have defined boundaries with barriers that provide sufficient delay time to impede, control, or deter unauthorized access.

(1)   MAAs must be located within a PA and must have distinct boundaries. Multiple MAAs may exist within a single PA; however, an MAA cannot cross a PA boundary.

(2)   While an MAA is required for the protection of Category I quantities of SNM, classified matter may exist within an MAA. In such instances, the classified matter must be stored according to the requirements in DOE M 470.4-4A.

b.   <u>Access Control</u>. Access control must be administered by armed PF personnel and/or automated access control systems.

(1)   Access must be controlled to limit entry to individuals with a Q security clearance and who have been authorized for entry consistent with need-to-know and operations.

(2)   Individuals without appropriate security clearance must be escorted.

    (a)   The cognizant security authority must establish escort-to-visitor ratios for the MAA.

    (b)   The escort must ensure measures are taken to prevent compromise of classified matter or access to SNM.

(3)   S&S interests, not in approved storage within an MAA, must be controlled by the custodian or authorized user.

(4)   Validation of security clearance must occur at MAA entry control points.

    (a)   If MAA access is controlled by an unattended automated access control system, the system must verify:

        1   a valid DOE security badge (badge validation must match the data assigned to the badge holder),

        2   valid security clearance,

        3   valid PIN, and

        4   valid biometric template.

    (b)   The identity and security clearance of each person seeking entry may be validated by armed PF personnel or biometrics.

(5)   Site-specific requirements and procedures for visitors must be developed and approved by DOE line management. The procedures must provide for the information described in Chapter II and Attachment 2.

c.   Entry/Exit Control Inspections. Security requirements for entry/exit inspections must be established by DOE line management and documented in the SSP.

(1)   A separate physical or electronic inspection of each vehicle, person, package, and container must be conducted at all MAA exit points.

(2)   Metal detectors used for MAA entry inspection must detect the test weapons listed in Chapter V.

CHAPTER B-II. ALARM MANAGEMENT AND CONTROL SYSTEM

1. GENERAL REQUIREMENTS. The requirements for safeguards and security (S&S) alarm management and control systems used in the protection of Category I and II quantities of SNM and installed and operational after January 1, 2008, are contained in Appendix D of this Manual. This chapter establishes requirements for integrated physical protection systems protecting nuclear weapons, components, and category I and II SNM. Facilities with Category I and II quantities of SNM, or other high-consequence targets as identified by vulnerability assessments, must have a central alarm station (CAS) and a secondary alarm station (SAS). All intrusion detection system (IDS) sensors must annunciate directly to CAS/SAS when an alarm point is activated. Systems installed after July 15, 1994, must, where feasible, use redundant, independently routed, or separate communications paths to avoid a single-point failure. The perimeter intrusion detection and assessment system (PIDAS) surrounding the PA must be monitored in a continuously manned CAS and SAS. In addition to the requirements in Appendix A for Category III and IV SNM, the following requirements apply.

   a. Central Alarm Station.

   (1) The CAS must be attended continually.

   (2) The CAS and SAS must be physically separated.

   (3) To avoid a single-point failure, systems for the protection of Category I and II quantities of SNM installed after July 15, 1994, must, where feasible, use redundant, independently routed, or separate communication paths.

   (4) The CAS must be designed as a hardened post, located within a limited area (LA) or greater security area and manned 24 hours a day.

   (5) Exterior walls, windows, doors, and roofs must be constructed of, or reinforced with, materials that have a bullet-penetration resistance equivalent to the Level 8 rating given in Underwriters Laboratories (UL) Standard 752, *Standard for Bullet-Resisting Equipment.*

   (6) Entryways must be fitted with doors equipped with locks that can be operated from within the alarm station.

   b. Secondary Alarm Station. The SAS must be used as an alternative alarm annunciation point to the CAS and be manned 24 hours a day so that a response can be initiated if the CAS cannot perform its intended function.

   (1) The SAS need not be fully redundant to the CAS but must be capable of providing full command and control in response to S&S events [see paragraph 1a(3) above].

   (2) The SAS may be located in a property protection area.

2.   <u>CLOSED-CIRCUIT TELEVISION (CCTV) SYSTEM</u>. CCTV assessment systems must be functional under day, night, overcast, and artificial lighting conditions. The system must provide a clear and suitable image for assessment.

    a.   <u>Primary Assessment</u>. When used as the primary means of alarm assessment and to determine response level, the system requirements are listed below.

        (1)   CCTV systems must annunciate when the video signal from the camera is disrupted or lost.

        (2)   The video subsystem must be integrated with the CAS/SAS alarm display systems.

        (3)   The system must have the capability to automatically switch to the camera associated with the alarm event and to display that event for operator assessment.

        (4)   Video recorders must be actuated by the intrusion alarm and record automatically.

        (5)   Video recorder response time must be rapid enough to record the actual intrusion, be able to capture sufficient information for alarm assessment, and have the capacity to store at least 45 days of "event logs" before archiving the information to removable nonvolatile media.

        (6)   Video assessment coverage must be complete (e.g., no gaps between zones or areas that cannot be assessed because of shadows or objects blocking the camera's field of view).

        (7)   CCTV used for primary assessment must be tamper protected on a 24 hour circuit (camera enclosures and the video and data lines) and use fixed cameras with fixed focal length lenses that provide a clear image for assessment (pan tilt and zoom cameras may be used for surveillance).

        (8)   CCTV systems must use real-time signal or near real-time transmission of camera views.

        (9)   The video system must accept manual override of automatic features. This capability permits the operation of a CCTV camera associated with another event.

    b.   <u>Additional CCTV Requirements</u>.

        (1)   When CCTV systems are used, the alarm control system must be able to call the operators' attention to an alarm associated video recorder/monitor.

(2)   The video assessment must be supported by sufficient lighting or other means necessary to facilitate alarm assessment.

(3)   The picture quality must allow the operator to recognize and discriminate between human and animal presence in the camera field of view.

CHAPTER B-III. COMMUNICATIONS, ELECTRICAL POWER, AND LIGHTING

1.   COMMUNICATIONS.

    a.   General Requirements. Communications equipment must meet the following requirements.

        (1)   Redundant Voice Communications. Facilities protecting Category I and II quantities of SNM must have a minimum of two different voice communications technologies to link the CAS/ SAS to each fixed post and protective force (PF) duty location. Alternative communications capabilities must be available immediately if the primary communications system fails. Channels considered critical to protective personnel communications must have backup channels.

        (2)   Records. Records of the failure and repair of all PF radio communications equipment must be maintained so that type of failure, unit serial number, and equipment type can be compiled.

        (3)   Recording of Communication. A continuous electronic recording system must be provided for all security radio traffic and telecommunications lines that provide support to the CAS. The recorder must be equipped with a time track and must cover all security channels. Sites must follow the established requirements for consensual Listening-In to or Recording Telephone/Radio Conversations (see DOE 1450.4, *Consensual Listening-in to or Recording Telephone/Radio Conversations*, dated 11-12-92).

    b.   Communication Systems. Protection system communications must support two vital functions: alarm communication/display and PF communications. PF communications include the procedures and hardware that enable officers to communicate with each other.

        (1)   Design Considerations. The design of a PF communication system must address resistance to eavesdropping, vulnerability to transmission of deceptive messages, and susceptibility to jamming.

        (2)   Protective Force Radio System Requirements. The application of digital encryption may be implemented on a graded basis. When the PF communications are converted to meet Federal Communications Commission (FCC) narrow band frequency requirements, digital encryption (see ANSI/TIA/EIA-102 Phase I, referred to as Project 25) must be included.

        (3)   Alternative Means of Communication. Alternative means of communication must be in place such as telephones, intercoms, public

address systems, hand signals, sirens, lights, pagers, couriers, computer terminals, flares, duress alarms, smoke, or whistles.

    (4)   Local Law Enforcement Agency (LLEA) Communication. A mechanism must be established to ensure communication with LLEAs. An alternative communications capability from a SAS must be provided if the primary station is compromised. Daily tests of these communications systems must be conducted with LLEAs unless a different rate is required by memorandum of agreement/understanding and is documented in the site security plan (SSP).

c.   Duress Systems. Facilities with protected areas and material access areas must have duress notification capabilities for mobile and fixed posts and for the CAS/SAS. The duress system must meet the following requirements.

    (1)   Activation of the duress alarm must be as unobtrusive as practicable. The duress alarm must annunciate at the CAS and SAS but not at the initiating PF post.

    (2)   The duress alarm for a CAS must annunciate at the SAS while the duress alarm for the SAS must annunciate at the CAS.

    (3)   Mobile duress alarms must annunciate at the CAS, SAS, or another fixed post.

    (4)   All PF fixed posts must have duress devices (see DOE M 470.4-3A, *Contractor Protective Force*, dated 11-5-08).

d.   Radios. Fixed-post radios, mobile radios, and portable radios must be provided to support operational security requirements.

    (1)   Radio System Requirements. The radio system must be capable of accessing security operational and support channels.

        (a)   Radios must have power and sensitivity for two-way voice communications with the facility base stations using the primary channel.

        (b)   Security communication channels must be restricted to security operations.

        (c)   Radio system components must be protected against destruction and unauthorized access.

        (d)   Radio programming consoles must be protected from unauthorized programming changes.

(e)   Radio systems components must be protected from physical damage.

(2)   Portable Radios. Portable radios must be capable of two-way communication on the primary security channel from within buildings and structures. An alternative means of communications must be provided if safety or process procedures prohibit transmission within a building or structure.

(3)   Two-Way Communications. Mobile radios and base station radios must be capable of maintaining two-way communication with the CAS/SAS on the primary channel.

(4)   Emergency Response Channels. Base stations, which are controlled from the CAS, must include emergency response channels.

(5)   Battery Power. Portable radios must operate for an 8-hour period at maximum expected duty cycles. Procedures for radio exchange, battery exchange, or battery recharges can be used to meet this requirement.

(6)   Repeater Stations. A radio repeater station must be placed in a location that ensures all-weather access for vehicles and personnel to the station building, antenna, standby generator plant, and fuel storage tanks. The station must be designed to minimize risk of damage to the antenna structure and supporting guide lines from vehicular traffic.

e.   PF Tracking Systems. Systems capable of tracking and displaying the live movements and state-of-health of PF may be used to improve the situational awareness of PF commanders. Data associated with these systems are typically transmitted by radio frequency so the following limitations apply:

(1)   Classified information may not be transmitted by the wireless communications associated with tracking systems.

(2)   PF tracking systems used at sites with Category I quantities of SNM must be evaluated prior to implementation by the cognizant security authority. The evaluation is to determine if the high system effectiveness rating, as described in DOE M 470.4-1, would be degraded, if compromised unless encrypted.

f.   Radio Frequency Alarm Communications. The radio frequency alarm communications systems, when used to protect Category I and II quantities of SNM, must be limited to emergency, temporary situations, or early warning detection applications. When used, a comprehensive risk assessment must be conducted and the DOE Graded Security Protection (GSP) implementation plan established. Radio frequency alarm systems and associated communication systems used for the protection of Category I and II quantities of SNM must comply with the requirements outlined for the protection of Category III and IV quantities of SNM and meet the following additional requirements.

   (1)   RF alarm communications systems are used for auxiliary security applications and do not require the same robustness as primary systems for protection of Category I and II quantities of SNM.

   (2)   Use of a RF alarm communications system must be evaluated prior to implementation by the cognizant security authority and determined to not effect a high system effectiveness rating as described in DOE M 470.4-1, if compromised.

2.   ELECTRICAL POWER.

   a.   Primary Power Supply. All IDSs protecting S&S interests must have a primary power source from normal onsite power. Early warning systems that have self-contained electrical power are exempt from this requirement. Power sources must contain a switching capability for operational testing to determine required auxiliary power sources. The following power supply requirements apply:

      (1)   Alarm and Communication Systems. Normal primary power must come directly from the onsite power distribution system or for isolated facilities, directly from the public utility.

      (2)   Communications and Automated Information Systems, Alarm Stations, and Radio Repeater Stations. Critical system elements must be connected to an uninterruptible power supply (UPS) or to auxiliary power.

      (3)   Radio System Centers. Power supply requirements must be determined assuming that all transmitters are keyed simultaneously while associated receivers and other equipment and building services are in operation.

   b.   Auxiliary Power Sources. Intrusion detection and assessment, automated access control, and CCTV systems protecting Category I and II quantities of SNM and/or Top Secret matter must have an auxiliary power capability.

      (1)   Transfer to auxiliary power must be automatic upon failure of the primary source and must not affect operation of the protection system, subcomponents, or devices.

      (2)   The CAS and SAS must receive an alarm indicating failure of the protection system's primary power and immediately transfer to the auxiliary power source.

      (3)   When used, rechargeable batteries must be kept fully charged or subject to automatic recharging whenever the voltage drops to a level specified by the battery manufacturer. Non-rechargeable batteries must be replaced based on manufacturer's recommendations. The system must be capable

of generating a low-battery alarm which shall be transmitted to the CAS and SAS.

    (4)   Power sources must have the necessary built-in features to facilitate periodic operational testing to verify their readiness.

    c.   <u>Uninterruptible Power Sources</u>. UPS must be provided for systems requiring continuous power and considered for systems that, if interrupted, would degrade the protection of the associated security area.

3.   <u>LIGHTING</u>.

    a.   Lights must support a 24-hour visual assessment and provide, as a minimum, 2 foot-candle illumination at ground level for at least a 30-feet (9.14-meters) diameter around PF posts and a minimum of 0.2-foot candle illumination within the PIDAS isolation zone.

    b.   Sufficient lighting for assessment must be maintained on the PIDAS sensor zones and the clear zones for CCTV assessment and surveillance 24 hours a day. The lighting must complement the CCTV system in supporting its video assessment capability.

    c.   Where protective lighting at remote locations is not feasible, PF patrols and/or fixed posts must be equipped with night-vision and/or thermal imaging devices. Night-vision and/or thermal imaging devices should not be used routinely in lieu of protective lighting at entrances and exits but may be used if lighting is lost.

    d.   Light glare must be minimized.

    e.   Light sources on protected perimeters must be located so that illumination is directed outward so that the PF is not blinded or silhouetted.

    f.   When back-up emergency lighting is used, it must be periodically tested to ensure that it will function as configured for a specified sustained period.

CHAPTER B-IV. INTRUSION DETECTION AND ASSESSMENT SYSTEMS

1. <u>GENERAL REQUIREMENTS</u>. Nuclear weapons and Category I and II quantities of SNM must be protected by an integrated physical protection system using protective force, barriers, and Intrusion Detection and Assessment Systems (IDAS).

    a. <u>Protecting SNM</u>. The following requirements apply for alarms protecting Category I and II quantities of SNM.

        (1) Interior or exterior Intrusion Detection and Assessment Systems (IDASs) must be designed with independent, redundant data communication lines.

        (2) Intrusion detection and assessment must be immediate.

        (3) Video signal protection would include video signal encryption for conditions wherein video coverage cannot be masked from viewing classified matter.

    b. <u>Early Warning Intrusion Detection</u>. Sites may use early warning intrusion detection to supplement their PIDAS as a means of achieving increased adversary detection and improved overall system performance. The false and nuisance alarm rates, degradation, and detection area maintenance requirements of a PIDAS do not apply to early warning systems. Each individual early warning or extended range exterior intrusion detection sensor must have false and nuisance alarm rates that do not degrade the overall effectiveness of the system, including monitoring personnel's ability to assess and manage alarms, and be documented in the site security plan (SSP).

2. <u>EXTERIOR INTRUSION DETECTION SYSTEM</u>. Exterior IDASs are designed to detect unauthorized entry into security areas.

    a. <u>Exterior IDS</u>. The location of communication lines must be documented in the SSP consistent with Table A-1, Line Supervision Protection (see Chapter A-IX of the base Manual).

        (1) Intrusion detection and assessment systems must function effectively in all environmental conditions and under all types of lighting conditions or compensatory measures must be implemented.

        (2) PIDAS must use multilayered, complementary intrusion detection sensors.

    b. <u>Detection Capability</u>. A PIDAS must be capable of detecting an individual crossing the detection zone by walking, crawling, jumping, running, rolling, or climbing the fence at any point in the detection zone, with a detection probability of 90 percent and confidence level of 95 percent. Performance testing should be conducted to determine the proper settings for high detection rates with the lowest possible nuisance alarm rates. Tests should be performed with a low-profile target (crawling) and a higher velocity and profile targets (walking, running, fast-crawl, rolling). Whenever practical, the tests should be conducted under the sort of adverse weather and lighting conditions that are common to the local environment.

(1)   The IDS must be tested when installed and annually (at least every 12 months) thereafter to validate that it meets detection probability and confidence level requirements.

(2)   Any time the IDS falls below the required probability of detection, the IDS must be repaired and retested.

(3)   When calculating detection probability for multiple sensor systems, detection is assumed if any of the sensors report an intrusion.

(4)   Additional operability and effectiveness testing must be conducted and documented in the SSP (see DOE M 470.4-1).

c.   Perimeter Intrusion Detection and Assessment System. The PIDAS surrounding the protected area must be monitored in a continuously manned central alarm station and a secondary alarm station. PIDAS must be:

(1)   designed to cover the entire perimeter without a gap in detection, including the walls and roofs of structures situated within the designated security area;

(2)   located such that the length of each detection zone is consistent with the characteristics of the sensors used in that zone and the topography;

(3)   designed, installed, and maintained to prevent adversaries from circumventing the detection system;

(4)   systems installed after July 15, 1994, must, where economically feasible, use redundant, independently routed, or separate communication paths, to avoid a single-point failure;

(5)   provided with an isolation zone at least 20-feet (6-meters) wide and clear of fabricated or natural objects that would interfere with operation of detection systems or the effectiveness of the assessment; and

(6)   free of wires, piping, poles, and similar objects that could be used to assist an intruder traversing the isolation zone or that could assist in the undetected ingress or egress of an adversary or matter.

d.   PIDAS Zone Degradation. Each PIDAS detection zone must be kept free of snow, ice, grass, weeds, debris, wildlife, and any other item that may degrade the effectiveness of the system. When this cannot be accomplished and detection capabilities become degraded, compensatory measures must be taken.

e.   <u>Preventive Maintenance</u>. PIDAS, security area and other security lighting, and security system-related emergency power or auxiliary power supplies must be included in a preventive maintenance program.

CHAPTER B-V. ACCESS CONTROLS AND ENTRY/EXIT INSPECTIONS

1. ACCESS CONTROL SYSTEMS AND ENTRY CONTROL POINTS. Entry control points must be located within the PIDAS and protected by the PIDAS when not in use. This configuration must provide a continuous PIDAS zone at the barrier that encompasses the entry control point. The entry control point should permit entry of only one person at a time into PAs and MAAs. Electronic entry control point search equipment (e.g., metal detectors) must annunciate locally to a protective force-staffed entry control point instead of annunciating at the CAS and SAS.

2. AUTOMATED ACCESS CONTROL SYSTEMS. Automated access control systems may be used in place of or in conjunction with protective or other authorized personnel to meet access requirements.

    a. Both the CAS and SAS must monitor the automated access control system's intrusion alarm events.

    b. Badge readers at PAs and MAAs must have anti-passback protection.

3. ENTRY/EXIT INSPECTIONS. Entry/exit inspections are required at Pas and MAAs, and at other security areas as required by DOE line management and documented in the SSP.

    a. Entry inspections of personnel, hand-carried items, packages, and/or vehicles must ensure prohibited articles are detected and are not introduced without authorization.

    b. Exit inspections must ensure S&S interests are not removed without authorization.

4. EMERGENCY PERSONNEL AND VEHICLES. Emergency personnel and vehicles may be authorized for immediate entry to security areas in response to an emergency if conditions and procedures for immediate entry are documented in the SSP.

    a. The protective force (PF) or other designated site personnel must maintain continuous surveillance of all emergency vehicles that enter the site.

    b. Arrangements must be made to inspect emergency personnel and vehicles when exiting after the emergency is over or when leaving the site. If the emergency condition prevents an exit inspection before departing the site, an escort must be provided, and both personnel and emergency vehicles must be inspected as soon as the emergency is over.

CHAPTER B-VI. SECURE STORAGE

1. SPECIAL NUCLEAR MATERIAL VAULT. An SNM vault must be a
    penetration-resistant enclosure that has doors, walls, floor, and roof/ceiling designed and
    constructed to significantly delay penetration from forced entry and equipped with
    intrusion detection system devices on openings allowing access. The material thickness
    must be determined by the requirement for forcible entry delay times for the safeguards
    and security interests stored within, but must not be less than the delay time provided by
    a minimum 8-inch (20.32-centimeters)-thick reinforced concrete poured in place with a
    28-day compressive strength of 2,500 pounds per square inch (17,237 kilopascal).
    Activated technologies such as activated barriers or passive/active denial systems may be
    used in lieu of thicker concrete when analysis indicates that delay times exceeding that of
    8-inch (20.32-centimeters)-thick reinforced concrete are required. The site's analysis of
    the protection measures in use must be documented in the site security plan.

2. VAULT DOOR. A vault door and frame must meet the General Services
    Administration's (GSA's) highest level of penetration resistance. The lock on the door
    must be a minimum of a GSA-approved Federal Supply Schedule-listed high-security
    lock, as described in Chapter VIII of this CRD.

3. WALL PENETRATIONS. Any openings of a size and shape to permit unauthorized
    entry (larger than 96 square inches [619.2 square centimeters] in area and more than
    6 inches [15.24 centimeters] in its smallest dimension) must be equipped with the
    measures described in Chapter VIII of the base CRD.

CHAPTER B-VII. PROTECTIVE FORCE POSTS

1. <u>PROTECTIVE FORCE (PF) POSTS</u>.

    a. <u>Special Nuclear Material Access</u>. Permanent PF posts controlling access to protected areas and material access areas must be constructed to meet the requirements for a hardened post. Exterior walls, windows, roofs, and doors must be constructed of, or reinforced with, materials that have a bullet-penetration resistance equivalent to the Level 8 high-power rifle rating given in Underwriters Laboratory (UL) *Standard for Bullet Resisting Equipment*.

    b. <u>PF Towers</u>. PF towers intended to be used as tactical fighting positions must have, as a minimum, a bullet-penetration resistance equivalent to the Level 8 high-power rifle rating given in UL-752, *Standard for Bullet Resisting Equipment*.

    c. <u>Fighting Positions</u>. Designated fighting positions must be sited in locations that command significant fields of fire and must be able to serve as bases of maneuver for PF tactical units. These positions must, as a minimum, have a bullet-penetration resistance equivalent to .50 caliber armor piercing.

2. <u>RESPONSE CAPABILITY</u>. A response capability will be used to deny, neutralize, contain, and/or perform recapture/recovery and pursuit missions within the required timelines (see DOE M 470.4-3A Chg 1, *Protective Force,* dated 8-26-05).

CHAPTER B-VIII. BARRIERS

1. GENERAL REQUIREMENTS.

    a. Barriers must be used to facilitate effective, economical use of protective personnel while maximizing their tactical posture.

    b. Barriers must be used to direct the flow of personnel and vehicular traffic through designated entry control points to permit efficient operation of access controls and entry point inspections and to provide PFs the ability to identify and engage adversaries along all feasible pathways.

    c. A clear zone must be provided along each side of security fences to facilitate intrusion detection and assessment. Double fences should be separated by a clear zone of at least 20 feet (6 m).

    d. The barrier design must deter or prevent an insider from diverting S&S interests past the barrier for retrieval.

2. PENETRATION OF SECURITY AREA BARRIERS. In addition to the requirements for a limited area, penetration of security area barrier requirements for a PA includes the following:

    a. Overhead utilities must not allow for access into a PA or higher security area without physical protection features to prevent or detect unauthorized access into the security area.

    b. Two permanent, continuous parallel fences (requirement for the perimeter intrusion detection and assessment system) must identify the boundary of the PA.

    c. Barrier requirements for a material access area include those required for a PA in addition to the following:

        (1) Barriers must delay or deter the unauthorized movement of SNM while allowing access by authorized personnel and material movement through entry control points and emergency evacuation as necessary.

        (2) Doors at entry control points such as transfer locations must be alarmed, and the alarms must communicate with the central alarm station/ secondary alarm station when an unauthorized exit occurs.

        (3) PF response time to an intrusion alarm must be less than the delay time that can be demonstrated from the time an alarm is activated at the PA boundary until the task is completed.

        (4) Penetrations in the floors, walls, or ceilings for piping, heating, venting, air conditioning, or other support systems must not create accessible paths that could facilitate the removal or diversion of S&S interests. Exits

designed for emergency evacuation must be alarmed with an intrusion detection system or controlled at all times.

3.   <u>BARRIERS-DELAY MECHANISMS</u>. Mechanisms must be used to deter and delay access, removal, or unauthorized use of Category I and II quantities of SNM and nuclear weapons.

    a.   Delay mechanisms may include both passive physical barriers (e.g., walls, ceilings, floors, windows, doors, and security bars) and activated barriers (e.g., sticky foam, pop-up barriers, cold smoke and high-intensity sound). The appropriate delay mechanisms must be used at site-specified target locations to reduce reliance on PF recapture/recovery operations.

    b.   Active and passive denial systems will be deployed, as appropriate, to reduce reliance on recapture operations.

4.   <u>ACTIVATED BARRIERS, DETERRENTS, AND OBSCURANTS</u>. If used, activated barrier and deterrent systems must meet site-specific requirements when deployed at improvised nuclear device/radiological dispersal device denial target locations. Activated barriers, deterrents, and obscurants must meet the following requirements:

    a.   Obscurants must consider spatial density versus time to deploy as determined by vulnerability analysis.

    b.   Dispensable materials must be individually evaluated for effectiveness of delay.

    c.   Controls and dispensers must be protected from tampering and must not be collocated.

5.   <u>VEHICLE BARRIERS</u>. Vehicle barriers must be used to preclude, deter, and where necessary, prevent penetration into security areas when such access cannot otherwise be controlled.

    a.   At Category I/II facilities, all potential vehicle approach routes to identified target areas must have barriers installed that will preclude an adversary from reaching the target.

    b.   If required by vehicle barrier design limits, speed reducers must be used to slow adversary vehicles to achieve site-specific threat/target system response requirements.

    c.   These requirements must be consistent with the operation of the facility and protection goals as documented in the vulnerability analysis.

CHAPTER B-IX. PROTECTION DURING TRANSPORTATION

1. <u>GENERAL REQUIREMENTS</u>. This chapter defines requirements for the transportation of Category I and II SNM. Packages or containers containing SNM must be sealed with tamper-indicating devices.

2. <u>OFFSITE SHIPMENT</u>. Offsite shipment of fissile nuclear materials of national security interest Category I and II quantities of SNM must be transported within the Transportation Safeguards System as addressed in DOE O 460.2A, *Departmental Materials Transportation and Packaging Management*. Specific items included in this policy are nuclear explosives, nuclear explosive components, special assemblies, sub-critical test devices, trainers, bulk fissile nuclear materials, and truck-transported naval fuel elements.

3. <u>ONSITE SHIPMENTS</u>. Movements of SNM between protected areas at the same site or between protected areas and staging areas on the same site must be escorted by armed protective force escorts.

CHAPTER B-X. MAINTENANCE

1. <u>MAINTENANCE</u>. Maintenance must be performed on site-determined critical and non-critical system elements.

   a. <u>Compensatory Measures</u>. Compensatory measures must be implemented immediately when any part of the critical system element protecting Category I and II quantities of SNM, is out of service. Compensatory measures must be continued until maintenance is complete and the critical system is back in service.

   b. <u>Corrective Maintenance within 24 Hours</u>. Corrective maintenance must be initiated within 24 hours of receiving a report that there has been a malfunction of a site-determined critical system element protecting Category I and II quantities of SNM.

   c. <u>Corrective Maintenance within 72 Hours</u>. Corrective maintenance must be initiated within 72 hours of detection of a malfunction for all other protection system elements protecting Category I and II SNM.

   d. <u>Non-Critical Systems Maintenance</u>. For non-critical system elements, the cognizant security authority must approve compensatory measure implementation procedures.

2. <u>PREVENTIVE MAINTENANCE</u>. Preventive maintenance must be performed on critical subsystems and components in accordance with manufacturers' specifications and/or local procedures.

3. <u>MAINTENANCE PERSONNEL SECURITY CLEARANCES</u>. Personnel who test, maintain, or service critical system elements must have security clearances consistent with the S&S interest being protected.

   a. Security clearances are not required when such testing and maintenance are performed as bench services away from the security area.

   b. Systems or critical system elements bench-tested or maintained away from the security area by personnel without the appropriate security clearances must be inspected and operationally tested by qualified and cleared personnel before being returned to service.

   c. Personnel who test, maintain, or service non-critical system elements must have security clearances consistent with the S&S interest being protected as determined by the cognizant security authority.

4. <u>TESTING AND MAINTENANCE OF SCREENING EQUIPMENT</u>. Screening equipment can include explosive detectors, metal detectors, x-ray systems, and SNM detectors and must ensure that prohibited and controlled articles are detected before being permitted into Department of Energy facilities.

a.   The following should be used as standard test weapons or the site must implement the performance testing procedures and test objects cited in Sections 5.1, 5.2 and the portion of 5.3 of NIJ Standard 0601.02, Law Enforcement and Corrections Standards and Testing Program, relating to non-ferromagnetic stainless steel knives:

  (1)   steel and aluminum alloy .25 caliber automatic pistol manufactured in Italy by Armi Tanfoglio Giuseppe, sold in the United States by Excam as Model GT27B and by F.I.E. as the Titan (weight: about 343 grams); or

  (2)   aluminum, model 7, .380 caliber Derringer manufactured by American Derringer Corporation (weight: about 200 grams); and

  (3)   stainless steel 0.22 caliber long rifle mini-revolver, manufactured by North American Arms (weight: approximately 129 grams).

b.   X-ray machines may be used to supplement metal detectors and protective personnel hand searches for prohibited and controlled articles.

  (1)   X-ray machines must provide a discernable image of prohibited and controlled articles.

  (2)   X-ray machines must image an unobstructed (discernable) set of wires and other objects as described in American Society for Testing and Materials (ASTM) standard for test objects (see ASTM Standard F792-01e2, *Standard Practice for Evaluating the Imaging Performance of Security X-ray Systems*).

c.   SNM detectors used in the inspection process must be tested using trace elements that depict the type of material located within the security area. The testing should provide for the identification of detection thresholds for the prohibited/controlled articles. The thresholds must be consistent with the SNM type, form, quantity, attractiveness level, site, configuration, portability, and credible diversion amounts of articles or property contained within the area.

5.   RECORD KEEPING.

a.   Testing and maintenance records must be retained in accordance with the requirements of approved records management procedures.

b.   Records of the failure and repair of all communications equipment must be maintained so that type of failure, unit serial number, and equipment type can be compiled.

APPENDIX C. SAFEGUARDS AND SECURITY ALARM MANAGEMENT AND CONTROL SYSTEMS (SAMACS)

The requirements for Safeguards and Security Alarm Management and Control Systems used in protection of Category I and II quantities of special nuclear material and installed and operational after January 1, 2008, are provided in Appendix C, which contains unclassified controlled nuclear information and will be issued separately from this Manual. This document has not been revised since it was originally published on 8-26-05. A copy of Appendix C may be obtained by contacting the Office of Security Policy at 301-903-6209.

DOE SECURITY BADGE PROGRAM

1. <u>GENERAL REQUIREMENTS</u>. DOE security badges issued to Federal and contractor employees have been determined to be the Department's Federal Agency identity credential. Within the DOE, a Homeland Security Presidential Directive-12 (HSPD-12) credential, hereafter referred to as the DOE security badge, must be issued to and worn by all DOE and contractor personnel (cleared and specified uncleared personnel, as further detailed below) who require access to DOE facilities. The DOE security badge is to replace the existing DOE standard security badge. Existing DOE standard security badges may be used until the new DOE security badge has been completely implemented within DOE. The DOE implementation of the new DOE security badge requirements are based on the Personal Identity Verification (PIV) guidance issued by DOE Notice or its successor (see DOE N 206.4). A local site-specific only (LSSO) badge is permitted for local site use. The Office of Science (SC) badge may only be used at specified SC facilities by uncleared contractors. The LSSO and SC badges do not replace the DOE security badge.

    a. <u>DOE Badges</u>. The following requirements apply.

        (1) DOE security badges must be issued to all Federal employees and cleared contractor employees and all DOE Headquarters (HQ) contractor employees who require long-term (greater than 6 months) access to DOE facilities or who have, or must have, a security clearance. LSSO badges may be developed and issued to address a variety of issues and unique local badging requirements including local site-specific access badge, temporary visitor badge, SC badge, foreign national badge, etc. These badges are not HSPD-12 compliant and are not recognized as meeting the requirements of the new DOE security badge.

        (2) Specifications for the new DOE security badge are described in National Institute of Standards and Technology (NIST) 800-104, *A Scheme for PIV Visual Card Topography*. The identity verification and issue process is described in a DOE Notice or its successor (see DOE N 206.4, *Personal Identity Verification*).

        (3) Individuals who are awaiting an L or Q security clearance may be badged using a LSSO badge. Once the security clearance is granted, the individual must be issued a new DOE security badge.

        (4) Individuals at SC facilities with security clearances must be issued new DOE security badges. The SC badge will not be recognized at non-SC facilities.

        (5) Employee identification cards must not be substituted for the new DOE security badge or any of the site-issued or foreign national badges.

b. Office of Science Badge. SC must prepare and distribute specifications for the SC badge. DOE line management must approve locally developed procedures for the issuance, use, recovery, accountability, protection, and destruction of the SC badge that are documented in the site security procedures. Designated SC sites that will not use the new DOE security badge are to be identified, and a listing of these sites is to be provided to the Office of Health, Safety and Security and the Office of Chief Information Officer. The SC badge can only be issued to uncleared SC field contractors.

   (1) The SC badge is not authorized for access to Departmental facilities that require the new DOE security badge.

   (2) Individuals at SC facilities granted security clearances must be issued DOE security badges.

2. TYPE OF DOE BADGE.

a. DOE Federal and Contractor Employee Badges.

   (1) New DOE security badges must be issued to DOE and contractor employees (including subcontractors) who have been granted a security clearance and who require access to DOE security areas or who have been subjected to an HSPD-12 identity verification and suitability determination. These badges must be used and accepted at all DOE sites and facilities (see DOE M 470.4-5, *Personnel Security*, dated 8-26-05).

   (2) Badges must be approved and authorized by the sponsoring site: Federal or M&O contractor organization/badging authority maintaining the badge holder applicant's identity documentation. DOE Agreements with other Federal departments and agencies for the processing, replacement, and turn-in of the HSPD compliant DOE security badge have been established in order to fulfill the HSPD directive. These arrangements must be documented in a procedure to include the provisions for the protection of the personal information.

   (3) DOE Federal and contractor employees (including subcontractors) granted a DOE security clearance must be issued the DOE security badge that displays the person's photograph and the security clearance level (L or Q). For DOE Federal and Contractor employees, the complete name (first name, middle initial, and last name) must be printed on the badge.

   (4) Military and other Federal department and agency personnel who possess HSPD-12 credentials/badges issued by their respective organizations and who are assigned/detailed to DOE will be issued a LSSO badge.

b. <u>Local Site-Specific Only Badges.</u>

(1) LSSO badges may be developed and issued to address a variety of local issues and unique local badging needs. This would include subcontractors, who do not require a security clearance or access to a DOE site or facility for more than 6 continuous months, without limitation on the contract performance period.

(2) LSSO badges include visitor badges, vendor badges, provisional badges, foreign national badges, and other site-specific badges designed and implemented to meet local requirements.

(3) DOE line management must prescribe or approve procedures for the design, issuance, use, accountability, and return of LSSO badges. LSSO badges must not resemble the design or color of the new DOE security badge or the DOE standard security badge.

c. <u>Visitor Badges.</u>

(1) Military and other Federal department and agency personnel who possess HSPD-12 credentials/badges issued by their respective organizations may, at the discretion of the DOE cognizant authority, be permitted entry to a property protection area (PPA) without further badging. If there is a requirement for entry beyond a PPA or access to special nuclear material (SNM), nuclear weapons, or classified matter, the provisions of paragraph 2.c(4) below must be followed. Even though the person possesses an HSPD-12 credential/badge, issued by another Federal department or agency, the DOE visitation process must be followed.

(2) Cleared visitors may be issued an LSSO badge if they possess a Q or L DOE security clearance or a Top Secret or Secret clearance granted by another Federal department or agency. Individuals with valid HSPD-12 credentials do not require re-badging with DOE HSPD-12 badges. Temporary/LSSO badges may be issued, if necessary. Classified visits must be conducted in accordance with the requirements of DOE M 470.4-1, Change 1, Section L, Control of Classified Visits Program. Prior to badge issue, the status of clearance must be validated with the granting department or agency.

(3) Military or other Federal department and agency personnel who are visitors not provided with new DOE security badges or their department's or agency's HSPD-12 credentials must follow the visitation procedures of the site to be visited. This may include a verification of identity, security clearance, employment status, purpose, and duration of visit.

(4) Visitors possessing a security clearance who require access to a limited area (LA), protected area (PA), material access area (MAA), SNM,

nuclear weapons or classified matter must submit a DOE F 5631.20, "Request for Visit or Access Approval" (see DOE M 470.4-1, *Safeguards and Security Program Planning and Management*, dated 8-26-05) prior to arriving at the site.

d.   <u>Temporary Badges</u>. Temporary badges may be issued to DOE and DOE contractor employees under locally approved procedures. Temporary badges must not resemble the DOE security badge and the DOE standard security badge. Depending on the badge equipment and technology employed, some temporary badge equipment may be capable of printing an individual's name and photograph. Temporary badges must clearly indicate that the badge is temporary.

e.   <u>Foreign National Badges</u>. Badges issued to foreign nationals will have a blue horizontal name bar with the individual's name printed on the blue name bar background. The badge should be processed as follows:

(1)   Cleared Foreign Nationals. Cleared foreign nationals may be issued DOE security badges. The difference between the cleared foreign national badge and the DOE security badge issued to U.S. citizens is that the individual's name will be printed on a blue name bar.

(a)   The foreign national security badge must be approved and authorized by the organization/badging authority holding the foreign national's personnel clearance file.

(b)   Cleared foreign nationals must adhere to the requirements in DOE O 142.1, *Classified Visits Involving Foreign Nationals*, dated 1-13-04 (see DOE M 470.4-1).

(c)   A foreign national may be badged at a DOE security clearance equivalent to their country's approved access level. The equivalent security clearance level should be based on the Government-to-Government Agreement and official validation by the foreign government of the person's clearance (see DOE O 142.1). NOTE: If there is no equivalent DOE security clearance level, the foreign national is badged as uncleared.

(d)   When a cleared foreign national with a DOE security badge, which is marked with a security clearance identifier, needs to access another DOE facility, the foreign national visit must adhere to the requirements of DOE O 142.1 and the provisions of DOE M 470.4-1.

(2)   Uncleared Foreign Nationals. Uncleared foreign nationals whose official duties require routine or regular access to DOE facilities must be issued LSSO badges.

       (a)   A foreign national badge may be issued for unclassified site access after an identity verification process has been completed by the foreign visits and assignments staff of the organization sponsoring the visit.

       (b)   Uncleared foreign nationals must adhere to the requirements in Change 1, DOE O 142.3, *Unclassified Foreign Visits and Assignments*, dated 2-21-08 (see DOE M 470.4-1).

f.   <u>Emergency Responders</u>. Emergency responders, designated by their organizations, will be issued DOE security badges. The badge will have the words "Emergency Response Official" printed on a red horizontal background. Emergency responders who are DOE cleared but do not have a need-to-know, or who do not possess a security clearance but gain access to classified material during the performance of emergency response duties, must have their identity recorded and receive a security briefing, by the Site Security Manager or designee, immediately following the emergency situation.

g.   <u>Non-DOE Emergency Responders</u>. Non-DOE emergency responders who do not have an HSPD-12 credential and gain access to classified material must have their identity recorded and receive the Site Security Manager or designee briefing immediately following the emergency situation.

3.   <u>ISSUANCE, USE, RECOVERY, AND DESTRUCTION OF DOE SECURITY & LSSO BADGES</u>.

a.   <u>Security Badge Issue</u>. DOE line management must prescribe local procedures for issuance, use, accountability, and return of DOE security and LSSO badges. These procedures must address the transition from the current DOE security badge to the new DOE security badge.

b.   <u>Issuer Requirements</u>.

    (1)   Issuance with Special Nuclear Material or Classified Access. Measures must be taken to ensure that a single individual cannot process and/or issue a DOE security or LSSO badge allowing unauthorized access into an area containing SNM or classified matter.

    (2)   Issuer Clearance Level. Personnel with read/write access to systems containing records and information concerning badges, security clearance, and access control authentication data must be cleared at the same level (L or Q) as the highest security clearance in the system data set. Sites must implement procedures to control access to security systems that maintain badging and clearance information.

c. Site Usage. A valid DOE security badge with a printed "L" or "Q" must be used and accepted as evidence of security clearance and must be accepted for admittance to security areas without additional security badging.

   (1) The organization being visited is responsible for verifying an individual's DOE security clearance level and determining need-to-know before granting access to SNM or classified information.

   (2) The information on the electromagnetic stripe, optical, or other data storage media must not be used for any purpose other than physical security and logical access control. The information on the electromagnetic stripe, optical, or other data storage media or in combination with biometric access control devices must not be collected or stored outside of DOE access control applications, without prior authorization along with established procedures for the control and protection of the information.

d. Thirty-Person Operations.

   (1) DOE security badges must be worn at DOE facilities and operations involving access of 30 or more Federal and contractor employees and who require a security clearance or who support DOE HQ.

   (2) Facilities and operations involving less than 30 persons whose contractor personnel do not require a security clearance or support DOE HQ are not required to have a DOE security badge. However, when uncleared personnel need access to a DOE site, building, or other than the HQs facilities, for no more than 6 months an LSSO badge may be issued.

e. Recovery of DOE Badges. DOE security badges are the property of the U.S. Government. Local procedures must be established for returning badges to the issuing office whenever an individual has terminated employment or their security clearance status changes or otherwise no longer requires the badge.

   (1) Individuals who no longer have a valid requirement for access to DOE facilities must surrender their badges according to local procedures as approved by the DOE cognizant security authority.

   (2) Badges issued to employees, contractors, and other individuals must be recovered at the final security checkpoint or earlier, and the individuals must be escorted from the site if circumstances or conditions indicate the need. Recovered DOE security badges must be destroyed and the records so annotated.

   (3) If a terminated employee's DOE security badge is not recovered on the last day of employment steps must be taken to recover the badge. If the

badge is not recovered, the badge must be treated as stolen Government property.

f. Individual Changes of Appearance. A DOE security badge must be confiscated and reissued, with a new photograph, if the individual's appearance has changed significantly; i.e., no longer resembles the person in the photograph.

g. Badge Destruction. DOE security badges that are deactivated or no longer needed must be destroyed so that the badge cannot be reconstructed. If destruction is not immediate, badges must be stored in a secure manner until they can be destroyed. DOE security badges must be destroyed in a manner approved by Federal Information Processing Standard (FIPS) FIPS-201-1, *Personal Identity Verification of Federal Employees and Contractors*.

h. Temporary and Visitor Badge Reuse. Temporary and visitor's badges that do not include individuals' photos must be recovered and may be reissued.

i. DOE Federal and Contractor Employee Name Change. A DOE security badge should be replaced when the employee's name is legally changed.

4. ACCOUNTABILITY OF DOE SECURITY BADGES. Records must be maintained by issuing offices showing the disposition of DOE security and LSSO badges. Such records must include the description and badge number; date of issuance; and name, organization, and date of the destruction along with a destruction certificate.

a. Records. Records must be maintained in accordance with the requirements of the local records management program. Personal data must be protected from loss or compromise (see 5 U.S.C. 522a).

b. Lost Badges. A record of missing DOE security badges must be maintained. Personnel and/or systems controlling access to DOE security areas must be provided current information regarding missing badges to prevent badge misuse. The theft or loss and recovery of DOE issued security badges must be reported immediately to the issuing office.

5. PROTECTION OF DOE BADGE MATERIALS AND EQUIPMENT. Stocks of badging materials, unissued DOE security and LSSO badges, and processing equipment must, at a minimum, be stored in a locked room, and locked filing cabinet/safe cabinet to protect against loss, theft, or unauthorized use. Security must be in place when the badge office is not located in a permanent facility. The cognizant security authority must establish protective measures for satellite facilities which are located outside a permanent facility. The cognizant security authority must provide guidance on the protection of LSSO badge stock and processing equipment. when located within a permanent and/or satellite facility. Thefts should be reported commensurate with the Incidents of Security Concern Program. (see DOE M 470.4-1).

6. <u>DOE SECURITY BADGE VALIDATION</u>. DOE line management approves local procedures for validation of the DOE security badge at access control points (e.g., by automation or protective force (PF) physical examination of the badge). Procedures must require PF or assigned security personnel to validate the DOE security badge at all DOE facilities, including those worn by pedestrians or vehicle occupants, and to ensure that the badge photo matches the presenter's face and that the badge has not been altered.

    a. Badge validation by PF or security personnel is not required at access control points that rely on automated access control systems for DOE facility entry/exit.

    b. Other methods of validation may be instituted employing biometrics, or a combination of personnel verification measures.

7. <u>DOE SECURITY BADGE RECIPIENT REQUIREMENTS</u>. DOE line management approves implementing procedures to ensure individuals receiving the DOE security or LSSO badge are responsible for the following.

    a. Protecting the DOE security badge against loss, theft, or misuse and reporting a lost, stolen, or misused badge to the cognizant security authority within 24 hours of discovery.

    b. Maintaining the DOE security badge in good condition and protecting its integrity by ensuring that the badge is not altered, photocopied, counterfeited, reproduced, or photographed (other than what would be deemed official government business).

    c. Returning the DOE security badge, according to local procedures and as approved by DOE line management, when it is no longer valid or required.

    d. Surrendering or returning the DOE security badge when requested according to local procedures approved by DOE line management.

    e. Wearing the DOE security badge conspicuously, photo side out, in a location above the waist and on the front of the body while having access to DOE facilities. (A deviation to this requirement may be permitted for health or safety reasons).

8. <u>DOE SECURITY BADGE-HSPD-12 REQUIREMENTS</u>. The requirements for the Federal government implementation of the HSPD-12 credential are described in FIPS-201-1.

www.ingramcontent.com/pod-product-compliance
Lightning Source LLC
Chambersburg PA
CBHW080244290526

45790CB00005B/1700